Revising the Person-Centered Approach

Pushing on the Envelope
But not very hard

Revising the Person-Centered Approach

Pushing on the Envelope
But not very hard

D. (Doug) William Bower

iUniverse, Inc.
Bloomington

Revising the Person-Centered Approach
Pushing on the Envelope, but not very Hard

iUniverse books may be ordered through booksellers or by contacting:

iUniverse
1663 Liberty Drive
Bloomington, IN 47403
www.iuniverse.com
1-800-Authors (1-800-288-4677)

ISBN: 978-1-4502-9270-2 (sc)
ISBN: 978-1-4502-9690-8 (ebook)

Printed in the United States of America

iUniverse rev. date: 2/17/2011

Table of Contents

Dedication

In 1987 I attended the first annual Warm Springs Person-Centered Workshop. I had the privilege to be among the students working with Jerold Bozarth from the University of Georgia counseling psychology department who helped plan the event. About 2 weeks prior to the occasion, Carl Rogers died. Nat Raskin, Barbara Brodley, Fred Zimring, Dave Spahn, Sam Mitchell, and Chuck Devonshire attended. Rumors were floating around that Carl Rogers' health was such that he would not be able to attend. No one expected to receive news of his death though. There was an atmosphere of sadness, but also optimism regarding the workshop and the future of the Person-Centered Approach.

I dedicate this work to my UGA peers who either helped organize the event or participate in it. These included: Dottie Morgan, Ann Schwartz, Carol (Top) Topping, Phil Barrineau, Joanne Cohen, Polly Payne, Howard Ellis, Elizabeth Strickler-Kirkpatrick, and Jeff Penick. Jeff's name isn't on the 1987 roster of attendees, but is on the 1988 list.

We have pretty much gone our separate ways even losing contact with each other. Dottie, Ann, Jo, Elizabeth and I still get to Warm Springs for the annual event. It becomes a reunion of sorts. Each has made a commitment to practicing the approach as they understand it.

Preface

"Pushing the envelope is what those in test flying do when they take their machine past the point where it has ever been before"

James Lovell

At one of the annual Warm Springs Person-Centered workshops, a psychiatrist attended who was interested in Eugene Gendlin's "Focusing." He was accused of not being Person-Centered. I considered the interaction with him as an attack. It felt self righteous and dismissive. It certainly reflected a narrow view of what it means to be Person-Centered. Over the years I have heard the charge "That's not Person-Centered" so many times that I cringe on hearing it.

In Person-Centered/Client Centered: Discovering the Self that One Truly is, I noted that "I keep pushing on the envelope of this approach." I am still pushing, not satisfied that I have captured the movement, the flexibility, or the different slant I want to address regarding the Person-Centered Approach. I want to get at the approach as a person to person approach free of legalism. I want to get at an approach that appreciates Carl Rogers, but doesn't depend on him. I seek to address an approach that is open to various interpretations of what it means to be Person-Centered.

In my own pilgrimage, I came to question the principles of nondirectiveness, nonjudgmentalness, and unconditional positive regard. I came to regard a rigid, uncompromising adherence to nondirectiveness as a form of directiveness. Come hell or high water, the therapist is to be nondirective. I found my colleagues in the approach to be every bit as judgmental as any group of people I associate with. On top of that I have known for years that I am judgmental and got tired of trying to be nonjudgmental. In addition, I experienced feeling judgmental with clients, even if I kept that judgmentalness to myself because Person-Centered Therapists are supposed to be nonjudgmental. Still, I saw those clients change though I was experiencing judgmentalness. Finally, sort of, I can't for the life of me figure out how positive regard can be viewed as unconditional. I found no criteria are available to determine if positive regard is actually unconditional. I certainly don't have a clue how clients can possibly determine if the therapist's positive regard is actually unconditional or just regular positive regard. Naturally, this impacts the so-called "Necessary and Sufficient" aspects of the Person-Centered Approach. Such questions do not undermine that a great deal of research has been done that demonstrates that the Person-Centered approach is at least as effective as any other approach. That also means that research as demonstrated it is not as effective. However, the effectiveness of all the approaches to therapy has been called into question.

Thus, I present this push on the envelope. I am simply saying to interested persons, be open to discovering the approach based on a personal frame of reference and the ability to interpret the approach. Adherents are not obliged to speak to or about the approach in such as way as to confirm to Carl Rogers' understanding of the approach. Adherents are also not obliged to confirm to the understanding that others espouse either.

Introduction: Highlights (More or Less)

This chapter entails a great risk, missing what the approach is about, while offering a questioning, and a view through my eyes. It occurs to me that dealing with the person-centered approach is rather like engaging modern art. The "eyes of the beholder" interpret and highlight what leaps out. And so, I present my views here, not as fact, nor as final word, but as a glimpse at how I see the approach.

Rogers a Snap Shot History

I am bias about this. I am convinced that the world around us has a major impact on our beliefs. I am sure I believe this because of what I have been exposed to myself from Freud to Whitehead to Rogers there would be support for this position. The slants would be different, Freud being deterministic; Whitehead being process oriented allowing for external influences while internal influences put their own unique twists, and Rogers allowing for more independence on one's personal growth through self-actualization. Still even Rogers who argued that human beings are basically good asserted that society creates or fosters bad behavior (Rogers, 1981).

However, in my bias I am not prepared to say just how Carl Rogers was influenced by the world around him.

Carl Ransom Rogers was born on January 8, 1902, the fourth child of Walter Rogers and the former Julia Cushing. Kirschenbaum (1979) wrote, "Carl was a sickly child – slight, shy, prone to tears, often the target of jokes and teasing by his older brothers" (p. 2). Kirschenbaum also indicated that Carl received a great deal of attention from his mother and siblings.

The family lived in a middle class setting in Oak Park, Illinois for a time and later on a farm close to Glen Ellyn, Illinois.

Of interest to me was that Carl Rogers was raised in a religious home with Calvinism and Fundamentalism being a foundation for the family religious practices. With Calvinism's legalism and Fundamentalism's rigidity, basic premises of Scripture would have been a part of Carl Roger's life as well as presuppositions of the Congregationalist tradition in which they worshiped.

Kirschenbaum points out the family spent a great deal of time together and Carl "spent his high school years socially isolated from his peers. Since dancing was not allowed for the Rogers, and that was what the young people mostly did at parties, he had practically no social life." Personally, I suspect it would be quite difficult to overcome shyness without having access to a social life. However, Carl Rogers did and it enabled him to reach out to the world through his theory.

China

In 1921, Carl Rogers was selected to represent the United States Y.M.C.A. at the World Student Christian Federation Conference to be held in Peking, China. Kirschenbaum quotes him as saying, "Surely God wants me for some great task, something that he is saving for me alone . . . Surely God's hand is visible in this last and greatest opportunity and responsibility that has come upon me" (p. 23).

During that trip his religious views were changed radically. To my knowledge Carl Rogers never again used the language above to describe a religious position.

However as a fundamentalist Christian myself, I keep seeing his Humanistic position as quite consistent with my own position. His position on nonjudgmentalness is actually closer to the Christian position than Christians might want to admit as Christ demonstrated concern about believers being judgmental. "Do not judge so that you will not be judged" Matthew 7:1 (NASB), comes to mind.

2

While there is often a great deal of emphasis in the person-centered approach upon Unconditional Positive Regard, the Rogerian notion of acceptance often seems to be to reflect the traditional Christian song "Just as I Am." And while the notion of empathy, entering into the world of another may not be directly found as such in the Scripture, and if it is I couldn't find it, certainly that principle is consistent with "Love thy neighbour as thyself" Matthew 22:39 (KJV) and with the Christian notion of the incarnation of Jesus who, "emptied Himself, taking the form of a bond-servant, and being made in the likeness of men" Philippians 2:7 (NASB). This image projects the Christ as one was willing to enter the world of human beings as if.

Surely, it is always dangerous to stand dogmatic in such statements. It may be like comparing apples and oranges. However, it does indeed strike me that attitude and intention are important components in these positions. Thus, I find the attitudes and intentions compatible

For whatever reason, Carl Rogers chose to consciously and deliberately reject the traditional jargon in which he was reared. That he did though doesn't mean that others raised in similar traditions have to.

New York

Newly married, Carl and Helen headed to New York City. He had decided to attend Union Theological Seminary over Princeton. Being biased that settings, people, and events influence peoples' lives, I can't help but wonder if the world would have ever heard of Carl Rogers had that decision ever been made. There is no way to know this as he did indeed choose to attend Union.

It appears here that any remnant of faith was purged by his studies. He shifted here to a more secular position. Exposure to courses at Teachers College at Columbia appeared to help solidify this secularization and probably further laid seeds for his theory and practice. He soon left seminary for the clinical and educational psychology program at Teachers College.

As a developing psychologist, Rogers took a Fellowship position at Child Guidance. Between his dissertation and his work there, I can't say there is much a hint of the theory that was to come. However, I can't imagine that Rogers didn't demonstrate the conditions he was to later espouse as being therapeutic.

Rochester

In Rochester Rogers appeared to be exposed to the realities of troubled children in relationship to available assessment and treatment. A position with the Child Study Department of the Society for the Prevention of Cruelty to Children exposed him to a multi-disciplinary team and a multi-disciplinary process of engaging troubled children. He even developed assessment instruments useful to the process.

However, I am convinced from my reading of Kirschenbaum that it was foster parents which may have been the most instrumental in moving Rogers towards his theory of helping. He in what appears to me as a glimpse of that to come Rogers is quoted by Kirschenbaum as saying that "certain types of attitudes" were important.

"1. An attitude of intelligent understanding . . . 2. A consistency of viewpoint and discipline . . . 3. An attitude of interested affection . . . 4. Satisfaction in the child's developing abilities." (Rogers, 1979, pp 73-74.).

These struck me this way, empathy, congruence, acceptance, and a basic trust or belief in the ability of the child to function.

Now I have to admit my bias. I am reading about and writing about Rogers having been influenced by the person-centered approach. And I also can not help but wonder how much of Rogers interview with Kirschenbaum was influenced by Rogers looking back through his own theory and thus recalling experiences and interpreting recollections through Rogers's present experiences being influenced by his own theory. A here and now theory does lend itself to wondering if past recollections actually don't say more about the present than the past. And so I

I also found myself wondering about Kirschenbaum's own interpretation of Rogers's biographical material. Writing Rogers's "drive toward health" Kirschenbaum wrote, "This "fundamental axiom," in my opinion, represents the basis of all Rogers' subsequent work after he left Rochester. Later on, some of his important work went into supporting his theory that human beings, like animals and plants, have an innate 'drive toward health' which can be nurtured by the right type of environment" (pp. 75-76).

I leave my revisit of Carl Rogers's "Rochester Years" (above) feeling that Rogers had experiences which had profound influences on the development of his theory and practice.

I found it hard to get away from the influences or Rochester. Above, foster parents demonstrated important aspects of relating that helped children. Later, Rogers was influenced by Samuel Hartwell who supplied genuine efforts to establish rapport with children. I certainly have to say there was a great deal of warmth concerning the brief descriptions about Dr. Hartwell.

Further, during this time Rogers apparently began seriously questioning the use of "persuasion" and "suggestion" during therapy. Allegedly he found that these methods were external sources of motivation. I assume that he noted that it was difficult to motivate children using these efforts.

Rogers then began having a loss of appreciation of a more interpretative methodology that he had employed himself. On one occasion while attempting to help a woman gain "insight" into the problems of her son, he reached a point of being flabbergasted and ended the session. However, the woman upon finding out that the Center worked with adults returned to her chair and began sharing deeply and profoundly her own experiences about her situation with her son. It seems to have had a major impact on Rogers and possibly contributed further towards his shift away from the models he had been exposed to. This shift seems to be related to another important theme in cct/pca, that the client knows what the problem is and is often, if not always, the best person to describe the problem.

As this discovery continued to unfold, Rogers was influenced by Rank. It appears that several aspects of Ranks theory were of interest to Rogers. However, the will of the client as a directive force in the client was one of the important slants. Also the attitude of noninterference and trusting in the client's ability to change and grow were important.

A rewording of his position led to the following for conditions for therapy: 1) Objectivity - the real demonstration of interest in the client without being taken aback by what the client presented or did; 2)

Respect for the client - accepting the client as the person he or she is; 3) Self-understanding - knowing the emotional and cognitive aspects of who the therapist truly is; And, 4) Psychological knowledge - being familiar with the behavior of human beings (Kirschenbaum, 1979, p. 96-97).

Ohio State

According to Kirschenbaum, it was during Rogers' time at Ohio State that he adopted two key words regarding this evolving approach, client, and nondirective.

The use of the word client appears to an effort to get away from the following model of a "patient." "A patient is usually regarded as a 'sick' person. He expects the doctor to cure him, to do something to him, to assume much of the responsibility for his well-being. The assumption is that the doctor, because of her training, can know, even better than the patient, what is wrong with him and can prescribe the necessary method of treatment" (Kirschenbaum, p. 115).

The term "client" was seen as a more equalitarian word as it indicated two parties interacting equally. Rogers "wanted a client to be able to come for psychological help – counseling or therapy – in much the same spirit that a client comes for legal counsel or consults an accountant or architect" (p. 117).

Before moving to the term nondirective, I want to share some responses. It certainly is true that patients are treated as described above. However, changing the word doesn't change that. Also, in order to qualify to be a patient in psychotherapy or counseling, one is usually a person. I do understand that there are psychotherapists for animals. Yet, traditionally a patient is still a person.

In addition, people coming for counseling and/or psychotherapy are in distress. They come to deal specifically with dealing with their psycho-social state. While a person going to an accounted or lawyer may be in distress, he/she goes to these to deal with matters of money, or matters of law. There still remains the atmosphere of "I know more about accounting or law than you do." So the word "client" actually doesn't remove the issue of expertise.

The other key word shift was the term "nondirective." The basic assumption of this term is captured in the following statement" "the counselor takes no responsibility for directing the outcome of the process' (Rogers, 1942, p. 115).

"Let it be said plainly that the concept of counseling set for in this book is by no means the only possible concept. There are other definitions of the counseling process, and other ways of defining the counseling relationship. Probably the commonest definition of the process is that the counselor discovers, diagnoses, and treats the client's problems, provided that the counselee gives his active cooperation in the procedure. The counselor, according to this viewpoint, accepts a major responsibility in solving the problem, and this responsibility becomes the focus of his efforts" (p. 115).

Of interest to me is that the so-called directive approaches don't call themselves directive. This distinction was manufactured by Rogers as a means to distinguish the approach he was espousing from the standard approaches of the day.

At this point, it is probably appropriate to present Rogers' 1942 views of the characteristics of nondirective counseling. 1) "It aims directly toward the greater independence and integration of the individual rather than hoping such results will accrue if the counselor assists in solving the problem" (Rogers, 1942, p. 28). 2) "This newer therapy places greater stress upon the emotional elements, the feeling aspects of the situation, than upon the intellectual aspects" (p. 29). And 3) "This newer therapy places greater stress upon the immediate situation than upon the individual's past" (p. 29).

Not sounding foreign to the later material on the "Necessary and Sufficient Conditions" Rogers (1942) presented 12 characteristic steps in the therapeutic process: "I. The individual comes for help" (p. 31); "II. The helping situation is usually defined. From the first the client is made aware of the fact the counselor does not have the answers, but that the counseling situation does provide a place where the client can, with assistance, work out his own solutions to his problems" (pp. 32-33); "III. The counselor encourages free expression of feelings in regard to the problem" (p. 35); "IV. The counselor accepts, recognizes, and clarifies these negative feelings" (p. 37); "The aim is to accept completely and to recognize those feelings which the client has been

7

able to express" (p. 39); (This is not at this point necessary an issue of valuing the feelings, but certainly of being open to what feelings are expressed for what they are); "V. When the individual's negative feelings have been quite fully expressed, they are followed by the faint and tentative expressions of the positive impulses which made for growth" (p. 39); "VI. The counselor accepts and recognizes the positive feelings which are expressed, in the same manner in which he has accepted and recognized the negative feeling. These positive feelings are not with approbation or praise . . . The positive feelings are accepted as no more and no less a part of the personality than the negative feelings" (p. 40); (It is my humble opinion that the latter concept of unconditional positive regard introduces "moralistic valuing" to this process and thus contradicts the objectivity of the 1942 position); "VIII. Intermingled with process of insight . . . is a process of clarification of possible decisions, possible courses of action" (p.41); (Here too, I feel that client-centered therapy moved away from this for fear it would violate the nondirective stance of the approach); "IX. Then comes one of the fascinating aspects of such therapy, the initiation of minute, but highly significant, positive actions" (p. 41); "X. . . . There is . . . a development of further insight – more complete and accurate self-understanding as the individual gains courage see more deeply into his own actions" (p. 43); "XI. There is increasingly integrated positive action on the part of the client. There is less fear about making choices, and more confidence in self-directed action" (p. 43); "XII. There is a feeling of decreasing need for help, and recognition on the part of the client that the relationship must end" (p. 44).

It would seem to me that these initial assertions were unbiased and have more freedom from presuppositions carried in the latter articulations of the approach. My own observations included there was freedom from unconditional positive regard and its ideals, the integration of empathy and acceptance into one condition without calling it a condition, and a sense of the process of therapy in relationship to the client's experience with that process. The initial assertions thus seem less idealistic and more possible than the latter assertions of Rogers following 1957.

Rogers' (1942) work described the "basic aspects of a therapeutic relationship." "There would seem to be at least four definite qualities which characterize the most helpful counseling atmosphere" (p. 87):

1). Counselor/therapist warmth and responsiveness.

2). Permissiveness in regards to the client expressing feelings and attitudes.

3). Giving the "therapeutic interview" structure ("There is the limitation, however, that he is not free to control the counselor.... (p. 89).

4). There is freedom from pressure and/or coercion from the therapist. ("Advice, suggestion, pressure to follow one course of action rather than another – these are out of place in therapy (p. 89).

Chicago

According to (Kirschenbaum, 1979), the years in Chicago "turned out to be the most prolific and productive period of Rogers' life" (p. 154). There was a host of direct and nondirect projects related to his theory and practice. There are too many to account for in this chapter. Summaries of Rogers' positions from Client-Centered Therapy (1951), and "The Necessary and Sufficient Conditions of Therapeutic Personality Change (1957) will be present which I hope are consistent in form with the presentations above.

An important statement needs to be presented here. "There is pending tendency to regard to nondirective or client-centered approach as something static – a method, a technique, a rather rigid system. Nothing could be further from the truth. The group of professional workers in this field are working with dynamic concepts which they are constantly revising the light of continuing clinical experience in the light of research findings (Rogers, 1951, pp. 5-6).

The reason I think it is important is because I believe a defensiveness and legalism set into this approach which has resisted revision of the approach. Movements like Eugene Gendlin's Focusing and efforts to speak of the compatibility of other theories with the person-centered approach such as Gestalt and Jungian positions have been met with hostility in person-centered community meetings. In addition, I lost count of the number of times I heard cct/pca practitioners charge each other with not being person-centered in their presentations and/or interactions. I myself upon questioning key concepts of the approach such as unconditional positive regard, nondirectiveness, and nonjudgmentalness have been accused in face to face interactions in person-centered communities of attempting to develop a new theory. The charges are not warm and often feel more like self-righteous indignation. Though, I certainly have to say they were human.

The point being that the approach seems stuck at times when people resist the changes based on the efforts of new people, and older adherents to speak of the approach differently because of their research and their personal experiences.

Rogers wrote, "In any psychotherapy, the therapist himself is a highly important part of the human equation. What he does, the attitude he holds, is basic concept of his role, all influence therapy to a marked degree" (p. 19).

In this attitude the counselor/therapist 1) Sets himself aside (p. 35) and "temporarily" divests him or her self (p. 40), in order to 2) endeavor "to understand" the client (p. 40). In this the therapist offers 3) "warmth" to which the client can "experience a feeling of safety. Here is the essence of "acceptance" (p. 41).

Another important statement needs to be presented here. Rogers wrote, "It has been our experience that there are many clinical situations in which it is genuinely difficult even for the experienced counselor to achieve the internal frame of reference of the client" (p. 43). I could not agree more. Yet it is precisely at the point of insisting on empathy that the approach falters. An attempt to be empathic all the time is a mistake failing to allow for not understanding. The genuine therapist is not going to understand everything the client presents. It may be doubtful if the client understands everything about his or her own experience.

This problem itself may be dealt with powerfully by the concept of acceptance rather than the concept of empathy/understanding. "When the counselor perceives and accepts the client as he is, when lays aside all evaluation and enters into the perceptual frame of reference of the client, he frees the client to explore his life and experience anew, frees him to perceive in that experience new meanings and new goals" (p. 48).

Perception certain is about understanding, but it is also about awareness which may have an aspect of the therapist's experience in relationship with the client that is not grasped at a cognitive basis. Instead of pushing on the client to become more understandable to the therapist, the therapist becomes aware that the client is having experiences yet to be cognitively understood by the client.

Here another part of the counselor/therapist's attitudes is important. 4) "To me it appears that only as the therapist is completely willing that any outcome, any direction, may be chosen – only then does he realize the vital strength of the capacity and the potentiality of the individual for constructive action" (p. 48).

5) "When the counselor has adopted in a genuine way the function which he understands to be characteristic of a client-centered counselor, the client tends to have a vital and releasing experience which has many similarities from one client to another" (p. 49).

I want to point out that Rogers did not write, "When the counselor has adopted in a genuine way the function which (Rogers) or someone else understands to be characteristic of a client-centered counselor, the client tends to have a vital and releasing experience. . . ." This points saves counselor/therapists from becoming clones and puppets of the approach and allows therapists to draw on their own perspectives and understandings to speak about what it means to be client-centered/person-centered.

At this point, I will not struggle at how far can this be pushed before one actually abandons the approach. Still the issue might not be all that dissimilar to calling one's self a Christian, Muslim, or a Jew while questioning basic doctrines and beliefs of the perspective religions.

Movement in therapy

I want to digress and briefly present several of Rogers' observations on movement or progress in therapy. I do this because I believe that this movement mirrors the essential qualities of therapy. If these qualities are present to a significant degree, movement will be noted.

1). "It was observed that though the individual first tended to talked about his problems and his symptoms for a majority of the time, this type of talk tended to be replaced, as therapy progressed, by insightful statements showing some understanding of relationships between his past and present behavior and between current behaviors" (pp. 132-133).

2). "Still later there seemed to be an increase in the discussion by the client of the new actions which were in accord with his new understanding of the situation" (p. 133).

3). "It was observed that while the client, at the outset of therapy, seemed to voice mostly negative feelings, there appeared to be a change in a positive direction" (pp. 133-134).

4). "The client's exploration revolves first around the various aspects of the problem, but gradually the concern is more and more with self . . . Not only is there movements from symptoms to self, but from environment to self and from others to self" (p. 135).

5). "Another trend in the content of the conversation is from material which has always been available in awareness, to material which until therapy has not been available to conscious consideration" (p. 135).

6). "Still another change in material is from past to present" (p. 135).

For more extensive statements on this I refer the reader to "Client Centered Therapy" (1951), Chapter 4 entitled "The Process of Therapy" (pp. 131-196).

At this point I turn to what I consider the focal point of this approach. I have to admit my own obsession with this material. I consider it both the strongest and the weakest. Strongest in the sense that this position powerfully represents what this approach to therapy and relating is about. The weakest, in the sense that such terms, as unconditional, have not been demonstrated as accurate, nor generated by the research. Also, the use of the phrase, "necessary and sufficient" has not been demonstrated as necessary and sufficient in light of the success of other therapeutic orientations. The phrase also is exclusivistic, that is, only those who hold certain qualities can really be therapists.

Carl Rogers (1957) in his article "The Necessary and Sufficient Conditions of Therapeutic Personality Change" asked "Is it possible to state, in terms which are clearly definable and measurable, the psychological conditions which are both necessary and sufficient to bring about constructive personality change? (p. 219).

I cannot say that his statements on these are clearly defined. As I worked on this project, I Found that I can not answer how it was determined that the conditions were necessary and sufficient. I also found that I could not and cannot determine how acceptance can be unconditional regard, or that unconditional regard can be determined to exist at all. Or further still how unconditional positive regard can be distinguished from conditional positive regard.

The Necessary and Sufficient Conditions

Rogers (1957), published what I consider to be the heart of client-centered/person-centered practice. Rogers (1980), to Bozarth (1998), consider the actualizing tendency to be the foundation block of the theory.

However, I disagree. One doesn't have to believe in the actualizing tendency to practice cct/pca. In fact, one doesn't even have to know about the concept of the actualizing tendency.

The key as far as I am concerned is a commitment to the "necessary and sufficient conditions of therapy. However, I am using the term "necessary and sufficient" loosely. I have no evidence that the conditions espoused below are actually "necessary and sufficient" for therapy.

Here are the (1957) conditions:

"1. Two persons are in psychological contact.

"2. The first, whom we shall term the client, is in a state of incongruence, being vulnerable or anxious.

"3. The second person, whom we shall term the therapist, is congruent or integrated in the relationship.

"4. The therapist experiences unconditional positive regard for the client.

"5. The therapist experiences an empathic understanding of the client's internal frame of reference and endeavors to communicate this experience to the client.

"6. The communication to the client of the therapist's empathic understanding and unconditional positive regard is to a minimal degree achieved" (p. 221).

These those are at the heart of the approach and have remained central to the person-centered position sense they were first presented.

Beyond Chicago

I am not going to spend a lot of time in this section. Whatever work was done on the formulation of the client-centered approach was done before the 60's. The research on the person-centered approach is more about affirmation and curiosity following the Chicago years.

Becoming a Person

This effort to help is deliberate and intentional though it does not dictate how a client should behave. Rogers asked this question, "How can I provide a relationship which this person may use for his own personal growth? (Rogers, 1961, p. 32).

Here is his answer:
1). "I have found that the more that I can be genuine in the relationship, the more helpful it will be" (p. 33).
2). "I find that the more acceptance and liking I feel toward this individual, the more I will be creating a relationship which he can use" (p. 34).
3). "I also find that the relationship is significant to the extent that I feel a continuing desire to understand – a sensitive empathy with each of the client's feelings and communications as they seem to him at that moment" (p. 34).

On Personal Power

Basic to Rogers' (1977) position is this statement: "the individual has within himself vast resources for self-understanding, for altering his self-concept, his attitudes, and his self-directed behavior – and these resources can be tapped if only a definable climate of facilitative psychological attitudes can be provided" (p. 7). My own position is that the client comes to me and makes me one of the resources. In this I differ from the traditional understanding of the approach which

14

reduces the range of therapist responses to empathic understanding responses which a advocated by (Brodley, 1992).

There is a new word here from the 1961 position, "attitude." Bozarth (1998), particularly used it while Rogers (1977) used the world "condition" more often than "attitude." Just what are these attitudes?

1). "The first has to do with genuineness, realness – congruence" (p. 9).

2). "The second attitude of importance in creating a climate for change is acceptance, or caring or prizing – unconditional positive regard" (p. 10).

3). "The third facilitative aspect of the relationship is empathic understanding" (p. 11).

A Way of Being

In 1980, Rogers again restated his foundational statement concerning the approach. "Individuals have within themselves vast resources for self-understanding and for altering their self-concepts, basic attitudes, and self-directed behavior; these resources can be tapped if a definable climate or facilitative psychological attitudes can be provided" (Rogers, 1980, p. 114). I am convinced that Rogers' concern about therapists asserting external control over the client was behind this. Yet, I find myself noting that the client makes the therapist one of those resources by coming for help.

Again Rogers offers the characteristics of the person-centered approach.

1). "The first element could be called genuineness, realness, or congruence" (p. 115).

2). "The second attitude of importance in creating a climate for change is acceptance, or caring, or prizing – what I have called 'unconditional positive regard'" (p. 116).

3). "The third facilitative aspect of the relationship is empathic understanding" (p. 116).

And with I'll stop. The conditions, or attitudes, will be described in more detail in later chapters. I will also share in those chapters more of my concerns about limiting the resources of the client to the client and ignoring the resources of the therapist. And I will attempt to get at why I reject just concepts as nondirective, nonjudgmental, and unconditional positive regard.

Finale

Dare I stop here? I have too. The approach continues to exist. Concerns have been expressed that it is losing its impact in the United States. However, reports from Great Britain, Japan, and Brazil from colleagues say that its influence is increasing in various parts of the world.

My own bias is that the approach rode the coat-tails of Carl Rogers and after his death has faltered. It didn't become a community approach and became too embedded in the interpretations of the approach from the past. It was a Rogerian approach, not a person-centered approach.

Efforts to assert new interpretations by new persons interested in the approach have been met with rejection of those interpretations as not being person-centered.

Thus, I consider the state of the approach in a stagnant condition. If new voices don't emerge with boldness, audacity, and courage, the approach will disappear. The trend of cognitive behavioral therapy and theory will prevail. The person-centered theory will disappear.

If those new voices do emerge, the humanity of this approach and its paradigm shift away from approaches which are mechanical, and prescriptive will offer significant competition for those who want a warmer, humane way of engaging others. It might be likened to the conflict between right brain function verses lift brain functioning. The two frameworks are different.

References

Bozarth, J. D. (1998). *Person-centered therapy: A revolutionary paradigm*. Ross-On-Wye: PCCS Books.

Brodley, B. T. (1992). Empathic understanding and feelings in client-centered therapy. *The Person-Centered Journal*. Athens, GA: Iberian Publishing Company, 1(1), 21-32.

Kirschenbaum, H. (1979). *On becoming Carl Rogers*. New York: A Delta Book.

Rogers, C. R. (1942). *Counseling and psychotherapy*. Boston: Houghton Mifflin Company.

Rogers, C. R. (1951). *Client-centered therapy*. Boston: Houghton Mifflin Company.

Rogers, C. R. (1957). The necessary and sufficient conditions of therapeutic personality change. In H. Kirschenbaum, & V. L. Henderson (1989). *The Carl Rogers reader*. Boston: Houghton Mifflin Company.

Rogers, C. R. (1961). *On becoming a person*. Boston: Houghton Mifflin Company.

Rogers, C. R. (1977). *On personal power: Inner strength and its revolutionary impact*. New York, New York: A Delta Book: Dell Publishing Company.

Rogers, C. R. (1979). Quoted in H. Kirschenbaum, *On becoming Carl Rogers*. New York: A Delta Book.

Rogers, C. R. (1980). *A way of being*. Boston: Houghton Mifflin Company.

Rogers, Rogers, C. R. (1981/1989) Notes on Rollo May. In H. Kirschenbaum, & V. L. Henderson (Eds.), Carl Rogers: Dialogues (pp. 237-239), Boston: Houghton Mifflin Company.

A Pilgrimage Towards Becoming
Person-Centered

I was first introduced to the Rogerian approach in nursing school at Manatee Jr. College (now Manatee Community College) in the late 1960's. My recollection is now foggy. However, it occurred this way. As I sat in class the instructor of the human relations course began a dialogue with another student. The student was holding a position that the approach was useless. As he protested, the instructor kept repeating the last things he said. After a few minutes, the student being flabbergasted sat down. He had suddenly realized he had been had. I believe he was trying to win an argument. It was impossible to win because the instructor kept repeating his assertions. The instructor had successfully illustrated her positions with her reflections. The student had been both defused of his objections while also being engaged in a way that he was allowed to express his objections. His feelings of frustration about the approach had been asserted. And then he was also allowed to experience being flabbergasted in his sudden realization that the approach "worked."

I was not impressed myself. I found the parroting superficial and felt the student was manipulated. I still feel that way about the incident 40+ years later.

I had entered nursing because I wanted to go into medicine and believed I needed to get a jump start on the medical knowledge. I did get that jump start. However, I was far more interested in fantasizing about getting into medicine than actually working at it. To this day,

I am still prone to fantasizing about a goal rather than working on it. Also, I am now convinced that I have an attention deficit disorder. I simply could not stay, and still cannot stay focused on materials for very long. Further, I didn't believe I was good student. That is, I didn't believe I could learn the complex material needed to get into medicine. And that may be true whether I have ADD or not.

My aspirations to become a physician however, were related to interests of going into psychiatry. I had developed an interest in psychoanalysis when I discovered Freud in junior high school. I actually developed a small reputation as an amateur analysis.

As I reflect on that now I am embarrassed by that reputation. There was a great deal I did not know. And I was very presumptuous in my analysis of others.

My model for psychotherapy initially was the psychoanalytic model which I held onto for many years.

When it became clear that I wouldn't get into medical school because of my grade point average, I developed an interest in going to seminary. On doing so, I studied further the psychoanalytic orientation.

When I completed seminary, I did a year of clinical pastoral education where I felt my experience with psychoanalysis was augmented by the psychodynamic twist to this approach. Dealing with transference, and interpretations of behavior, we often fancied our selves as being on target with our clever perceptions of the motives and behaviors of others. However, I was beginning to move away from the fixation and stage development issues I had seen in my readings. I was also beginning to doubt being shroud in my interpretations.

When I completed C.P.E., I began studying pastoral counseling. I was introduced to Theodore Lidz's book "The Person."

However, I was really beginning to find I was having trouble connecting with the in depth analytical models I was being exposed to. I simply did not grasp what my peers and the supervisors were doing and seeing in patients.

During my pilgrimage I was often found myself wondering what therapy was. At first, I thought it was about analysis and catharsis.

However, in 1982 as I worked on my pastoral counseling degree, I asked for a church in which I could serve full time, but have enough time to work on my graduate studies. I was appointed to Oconee Street United Methodist Church in Athens, Georgia.

While I was there I said to myself, "hey, the University of Georgia is right up the street. I'll apply as a transient student and take some courses to transfer back to the seminary." In the process of applying, I stumbled into the counseling department. I say stumbled into it because I didn't know the University of Georgia had such a department.

On acceptance to the university, I was assigned to Jerold Bozarth, Ph.D. as my major advisor. Because of that, I took his course on Theories of Counseling and Psychotherapy. Having the opportunity to look at several theories of counseling and psychotherapy side by side, I found that I best matched up with the Person-Centered Approach. Further, I was studying with a person who had adopted the approach and did not simply give lip service to the approach.

It was my "ah-ha" experience. I began radically moving away from the psychoanalytic type orientations. I wasn't really getting them anyway. I didn't mind and still don't mind dabbling in them. However, I really am not a good match for those approaches.

I found that qualities I long exhibited were regarded as therapeutic. I had long been able to be empathic, but simply did not really grasp that such a quality was therapeutic. I had long been able to accept others for who they were, though this was sometimes interrupted by a judgmental attitude. And in my C.P.E. experience I got in more in touch with myself and learned to assert myself. I believe that allowed me to be more genuine and congruent, and thus transparent.

The more I got into the approach, the larger my network became. I soon found Barbara Brodley, and by 1987 had added Nat Raskin, Fred Zimring, Chuck Devonshire, and Sam Mitchell. And I quickly added Bob Lee, John Woods, John Shlien and others into my network.

In pointing this out I am not saying I was becoming famous and seen as an expert concerning the approach. I was however, having significant interactions with many adherents to the approach. Further, I was engaging with several people in formal studies which led to my dissertation. And periodically I attempted to get published in journals on top of that.

I didn't master the article writing required to publication in peer reviewed publications. I simply had strong resistance to revising my materials. I didn't mind correcting grammar, but all too often I felt reviews were asking me to write a different article than what I had written.

Outside the approach, my writings were never received as adequate. My writing style was poorly regarded. And my content was often rejected as not containing anything new.

I thus turned to self-publishing. While I got a handful of articles published in person-centered circles, I created a journal so that I and others could be published. Not having a market for it, it quickly disappeared, but I received submissions easily. I also published two books and received submissions from others to round out the projects. This is my third project.

This project comes during a time of disenchantment with the approach. I have come to question the concepts of nonjudgmentalness, nondirectiveness, and unconditional positive regard. My questioning of these concepts has led to significant conflict with the traditional community. I have thus felt more like a heretic then an adherent. I find some comfort or courage in the history of Christianity which has its share of thinkers that were regarded as heretics. Martin Luther immediately comes to mind. And in the client-centered/person-centered community, Eugene Gendlin comes to mind.

I found from my interactions with the community a tremendous amount of judgmentalness within it. One of the manifestations of the judgmentalness was judgmentalness over being nonjudgmental. I also was very aware of my own judgmentalness and I got tired of trying to stuff it in the name of being person-centered. Further, I kept observing that though I was experiencing and seeing judgmentalness, I witnessed change and growth in others. Change didn't seem to have anything to do with judgmentalness. What was important was how the judgmentalness is handled, not whether there was nonjudgmentalness.

I also began to reject the term nondirectiveness as I saw the insistence on being nondirective as a form of being directive. The client had no say on whether I was "nondirective" or not. Further, I began to see that the approach itself essentially forced the client to accept the orientation of the therapist. While clients do seem to adjust to this style, they really had no choice except to terminate therapy and go somewhere else.

In addition, adherents to the approach were pressed by peers to be nondirective or at least appear to be nondirective. I recently received an email from a colleague who spoke about drifting away from pure or "classic client-centered therapy." The drift included becoming open to being "directive." Unless he had been taught that being nondirective is the framework for a client-centered practitioner should use, what difference would it make? It was clear that he felt he has deviated from being client-centered because he has become open to being directive. He learned that being nondirective was important from others who insisted it was important. Thus, he assumed that he had violated the approach because he was occasionally thinking in directive terms.

And then I really became disenchanted with unconditional positive regard. Closely related to the issue of nonjudgmentalness, I simply saw people badgered for, or accused of, not being person-centered. It was OK in this not to hold colleagues and peers with positive regard. And it was even interesting that colleagues and peers could be beaten up on for failing to hold the principles, but there were assertions that upr was being sustained while people were being badgered. Even as a peer was getting the tar kicked out of him or her, unconditional positive regard was said to still be sustained.

If that is what upr looks like, no thanks.

I also found that I didn't always have positive regard for my clients and others, but still found growth and change to take place. This change didn't seem to be related to regard.

As I challenged the concepts I found defensiveness from some community members, adherents of the approach that created alienation and even hard feelings. I often felt like I was engaging defenders of the faith.

In my pilgrimage I also simply did not find any protocol for determining that positive regard was really unconditional. To this day, I have not found such a protocol. Even if it existed, it could not stand scrutiny for it couldn't possibly cover all the possibilities regarding conditions that could be related to or thwart positive regard. Further, it could not really determine, save for the openness and honesty of the therapist, if the therapist was really really really being positive at all or assuming that role.

And many of the responses of feedback to my questions were, that upr is an ideal, if not a reality.

Other responses to my questions were met with claims that the issues I raised were not issues to them and people didn't understand why I simply did not accept the term without question. While others said, it really didn't matter if positive regard could actually be unconditional. They simply said that they chose to call this condition unconditional positive regard.

Many of the responses seemed odd to me in light of the Rogerian claim that upr was among the "Necessary and Sufficient Conditions" for therapeutic change. If they are necessary and sufficient, how could that claim be made without criteria for determining that pr was unconditional?

My own resolution can be simply stated. I have developed a concept of undistracted acceptance (addressed briefly in the chapter on acceptance). This position holds that in as much as the therapist or helper accepts the client or others as he or she is, receiving the client, therapy occurs. This position is not about warmth or positive regard. In fact, the therapist may not even like the client or other person in any given moment. Yet, the therapist/helper accepts this as part of the interaction and does not send the client/other away because the therapist doesn't like the client/helpee.

I feel it is important to say, however, that a therapist/helper may feel so negative about a client/helpee that it probably is a good idea to terminate the therapy. This may be a short term or long term experience with a referral, but a therapist should not continue to offer therapy to someone that he is beginning to have animosity and hostility towards.

The issue for me now is the issue of addressing my questions, however, thoroughly, or inadequately while still being open to trying to claim to be person-centered.

I liken my place now to being a Christian. Christianity is made up of Catholics, Episcopalians, Methodist, Baptists, Presbyterians, and a host of others. Christianity has survived the significant differences of opinion of what it means to be a Christian.

I hold that a good theory will both survive the slants that emerge from it, and generate new slants. The psychoanalytic theory did. Certainly the person-centered approach can as well.

If it cannot, it runs the risk of failing to be what it espouses, a phenomenological approach that is open to and interested in the perspectives others. If it cannot change when new people engage it and struggle with it, then it is too rigid to be helpful through the ages and will perish.

I push on the envelope myself. And sure I would like to be seen as a significant part of the revision, or reformation of this approach. Yet maybe at best I can encourage someone else to assert their perspectives on the approach while essentially being unnoticed. Even if unnoticed, maybe I can grant myself some grandiosity and self-deception to believe that my pilgrimage meant something to the general effort to articulate this approach.

I certainly note that in spite of my heresies, that I see myself as being person-centered whether or not more traditional adherents to the approach see me as such.

I certainly hope the reader will plunge into thoughtful examination of his or her own position and not feel boxed into expectations of conforming.

Self-Actualization

One day in late winter of 2006-2007, the neighborhood crows were noisily assembling. I stepped outside in an attempt to check on the commotion was. Not very far from the house, I came across an onion. It had deteriorated in the refrigerator, turning brownish and wilting. Appearing to be of no use to us as food we threw it into the wooded area in the front of the house as part of the mulch. Normally, fruits and vegetables continue to deteriorate there and add minerals and other ingredients to the soil.

To my surprise, sprouts were thrusting up from the center of the cut up onion. It had been through freezing outdoor temperatures, cut numerous times for sandwiches, and finally discarded.

The local high school baseball team I supported (Cedar Shoals), was struggling. We had not won a game. I shared my story about the onion. I expressed my amazement that under adverse conditions the onion was managing to survive. It was attempting to be an onion. The team was attempting to be a team and find ways to play good baseball.

The next day, I picked up the onion to put it into a container of soil. I wanted to see what would happen in a setting that was growth friendly. Even more to my amazement, I found the onion also had roots shooting downward into the ground.

On planting the onion in a pot, it continued to grow. After some time I checked on it again. Above ground it looked to be a "normal" onion. I gave it a little more time and pulled it up a couple of weeks latter. It had small onions forming at its roots.

After I told the story to the baseball team, among others, the team won several games and has developed more intensity, confidence, concentration, and improved its execution. Obviously, stories don't change abilities. The team simply started to find ways to be the best baseball team it could be. Somehow, attitudes of discouragement, puzzlement, bafflement, disappointment, criticism, blame, and a host of other oppressive attitudes began to change. In a hostile self-imposed environment, the team began to find ways to access the talent of the players. It began to change attitudes that would help it become more successful.

These to me reflect decent illustrations of what the concept of actualization is about.

Carl Rogers described self-actualization as the individual's "capacity and the tendency . . . to move forward toward maturity" (Rogers, 1961, p. 35). This process toward maturity enables an individual to move toward self-understanding, growth and change in such a way that his or her life will be enhanced socially, psychologically and spiritually.

In itself, this belief is not unique. Jeanne Catherine (2007) said, "Every person has this incredible mix of uniqueness . . . and it's a sad thing to see somebody who doesn't allow that uniqueness of themselves, that doesn't feel that uniqueness within themselves within their hearts."

Formative Tendency

Having reviewed this topic for myself many times over the years, I want to first describe it from my perspective. Then offer the perspective of Rogers. I am aware that in offering my perspective it is influenced greatly by what I have encountered on this topic through the years. However, I also have no doubt that I will put my own twist on the perspective (Jackson, 1981; & Whitehead, 1978). I also have no doubt that as I later describe Rogers' perspective, the effort will probably say more about my perspective than Rogers'. So if a person really wants to understand Rogers, I suggest reading Rogers.

The formative tendency is the tendency inherent in the universe for entities to form or take form. The universe has the ability to establish various kinds of entities such as electrons, protons, and neutrons. These form more complex arrangements working together as atoms. The scope of these arrangements is from hydrogen (H, atomic weight - 1.0079) to Lawrencium (Lr, atomic weight - 260).

Atoms in turn might combine to form compounds or molecules such as simple as water (H_2O) or as complex as DNA (Deoxyribonucleic acid).

Rogers (1980) wrote, "My main thesis is this: there appears to be a formative tendency at work in the universe, which can be observed at every level" (p. 124).

It now just struck me that he used the words "appears to be," and "can be observed" in the same sentence. It sounds rather ambivalent in light to these two comments.

Personally, I believe the formative tendency has its strongest support in the existence of the stuff of physics and chemistry. That particles (or whatever they are) come together to form atoms, molecules, and compounds or a host of substances is important. Thus the creating of forms is evident. They can be examined.

What the essence of this "stuff" is remains subject of debate. Yet, I see my car sitting out in the driveway and it is made up of "stuff." What may not be so evident is the basis of the forms. We cannot see electrons. We can only make observations of the impacts of electrons and aspects of atoms. There are particle theories, wave theories, and process theories concerning the essence of building blocks in the universe.

We can note that these come together and form a wide range of substances from oxygen which we breathe, to the planet "Earth." "It appears that every galaxy, every star, every planet, including our own, was formed from a less organized whirling storm of particles" (p. 125).

Even the notion of "entropy" which holds that there is a tendency for particles to break down, is part of the formative process. Is there evidence that what exists in the universe disappears? I think not. However, there is plenty of evidence that what breaks down actually changes form or reorganizes. That is, different forms emerge from previous forms. For instance when a star dies, it leaves different stuff in its place. There aren't any new electrons created as far as I know.

Former entities may take different forms. For instance, CO_2 may be separated into carbon and oxygen which might unite with other elements to form any compounds that contain these elements. Or maybe they will drift about through the eons as carbon or oxygen. Even if their basic parts (electrons, neutrons, protons, etc.) become separated, they still have forms. They might unite with others isolated basic parts to form the same element. Or they might form another common element if the conditions are right.

If there is a weakness to Rogers' position on this, it is emphasis on this formative tendency being optimistic. He seems to be in denial that in creating different stuff, old stuff is destroyed. In this, I have to suppose I have just joined him. However, in fact this destruction is devastating. In its extreme it could annihilate human kind and every other living creature.

Some of us don't find that a pleasant concept to consider. Optimism disappears with such destruction.

However, while Rogers seemed to highlight the positive aspects of this formative tendency, he also was realistic. "There are many who criticize this point of view. They regard it as too optimistic, not deal adequately with the negative element, the evil, the dark side in human beings" (p. 124).

I am one of those who feel Rogers was too positive. However, I appreciate Rogers' emphasis on the directional aspect inherent in the universe. It helps balance out the extreme pessimists who see gloom and doom in the universe. The opposite extreme of a positive directional process is equally difficult to adhere to. There appear to me both a positive and a negative direction to existence.

It has long seemed to be important to take note of the destructive and the creative aspects of that which exists. For even if I argue for a formative tendency, there is also the reality of death of stars, or the death of human beings. And if I argue for a destructive tendency, I also take note that forms often emerge out of something exploding or imploding. My own body may be carrying oxygen that was carried in the body of Albert Einstein.

Actualization Tendency

As above, I want to present my perspective on the actualizing tendency before offering Rogers'. I tend to view this as a more specific aspect of the formative tendency. I see it in relationship to living organisms. Simply defined, it is the tendency of an organism to come into existence. It is the tendency for life to be actual or be real. It has the ability to perpetuate itself and thus create new generations. I know of no evidence that any organism is able to sustain itself and keep itself going indefinitely. If organisms could do that, there would be a reduction in the need to spawn new generations. There would be no need for procreation in species that sustained themselves indefinitely.

Thus, there seems an inherent non-conscious aspect of living organisms to insure survival by replicating or duplicating.

The conditions for the actualization tendency are narrow. While there is speculation that there is life elsewhere in the universe, we only know of one place, earth, where life actually exists. Thus, the conditions under which life forms and is sustained is limited to situations such as those we encounter here on earth. The range of temperatures is limited. The content of the air, the soil, the water, and a host of others is limited that support life.

The actualization tendency is behind the vast diversity of life. It is behind the existence of life forms ranging from viruses to human beings. There is something about it that transcends existence as it creates the life entities that exist.

Rogers (1980) position is different from mine. Believing he was in sync with Goldstein, Maslow, Angyal, and Szent-Gyoergyi, his position concerning the actualization tendency was about movement of an organism towards maturity. "The organism, in its normal state, moves toward its own fulfillment, toward self regulation and an independence from external control" (p. 119).

I find myself wondering about the later part of this statement concerning "independence from external control." First, on the grounds it sounds more like a human issue. That is an issue of growth and development of a person in relationship to a social situation. Second, it is a human description concerning humans, nonhumans, or organisms. And third, even a superficial look at ecology demonstrates interdependence, not independence. There is no organism in existence that does not have a reliance on the environment or ecological system.

Further, all organisms make an impact on the environment. Organisms take from the environment and they put back stuff into the environment.

From the potato (Rogers, 1980), to the sea urchin, to the human being, the organism attempts at all levels to be what it is.

A significant mistake may be to think of this as a form of conforming to stereotypes of what the organism should be. For instance, all southern pine trees would be tall single trunk trees. Yet there are southern pine trees that have split trunks and others that have twisted trunks. In human beings we expect all human beings to have a fully developed brain with the appropriate level of intelligence. Such mythology has led to people with different capabilities to be prejudiced against and treated poorly for not having all the "faculties" of the prime examples of the species.

I have been amazed myself at the directional tendency in human beings when all vital systems appear to have shut down. I have seen people live in vegetative states for weeks. I couldn't see how they survived, but they did.

This was an extreme example, but I have been amazed at how so called handicapped children could find ways to touch people's lives with love, or turn people's lives upside down with powerful behaviors that tried the most patient among us.

I leave this section still believing in my brief review that the actualization tendency is a broader concept and is related to biology more than psychology. For the psycho-social-spiritual dimension, I personally believe self-actualization is a specialization of the actualization tendency.

Self-Actualization

Self-actualization is related specifically to human beings. It is the ontological, physiological, bio-chemical, and spiritual processes where by a self (a human being) becomes actual or real. It is the process whereby the human being becomes a self and "falls in existence" often attributed to Paul Tillich. However, I have yet to find a direct quote concerning Tillich making such a statement. One of my seminary professors, Ben Kline, used the phrase during a personal discussion with me and attributed it to Tillich. References to it can be found on the Internet but I can't find a direct citation. However, I like it for this theme of self-actualization.

Basically my most recent exploration of Rogers' position left me believing that he made little distinction between the actualization tendency and self-actualization. "Person-centered theory postulates man's tendency toward self-actualization. 'This is the inherent tendency of the organism to develop all its capacities in ways which serve to maintain or enhance the organism,' says Rogers (1959b, p. 196)" (Meador & Rogers, 1984, p. 142). If I wanted help with a Rogerian distinction between self-actualization and the actualization tendency, I would be hard pressed to offer one.

I have to assert in this that self-actualization is the process that makes a human being distinctly a human being rather than a gorilla or other similar animal. It is the process that enables our ability to think, to perceive our uniqueness, to interact with other human beings, and other creatures. It also enables us to create uniquely human creations such as cars, skyscrapers, monuments, and alter substances to make our lives what they are. In short, self-actualization is the process of creating a self.

Foundational Block?

According to Rogers, "practice, theory, and research make it clear that the person-centered approach rests on a basic trust in human beings, and in all organisms" (1980, p. 117). "The foundation block of person-centered therapy is the actualizing tendency" (Bozarth, 1998, p. 6).

I would agree and disagree. I agree in that every therapy is dependent on the capability of the human being to change or grow.

I would disagree in the sense that one doesn't even have to know of or believe in self-actualization in order to practice the person-centered approach. Thus, I would say the foundation of the person-centered approach is adherence to the necessary and sufficient conditions. Whether, I even believe in self-actualization doesn't matter.

It could be said that these behaviors (empathy, acceptance, and genuineness) are great models for troubled persons. Or, that they are tools for modifying the behavior of others. Or that they are of such high ethical excellence that there is no better way to relate to other people. Or one simply is good at holding these characteristics and sense it has been found they are therapeutic use them.

What is the Self?

There may be an audacity and a naivete in tackling what a self is? There certainly is inadequacy in doing so. No matter what I can say, it really won't be enough. Thinkers greater than me have addressed this issue and their efforts were left lacking. Yet, here is my own languid attempt at getting at this issue.

The self is a multi-factorial psycho-social-spiritual-biological phenomenon. It is what makes us distinctively human. In essence, the self is the unique twists on biology, anatomy and physiology, and neurology, that human beings have presented to creation.

While we share the characteristics of many other creatures, such as the ape family, the unique arrangement we have of those characteristics constitutes a human self.

Most particularly, our unique twist is related to the capabilities of the human brain or mind. The primary aspect of the self is the thinking experiential aspect of the person. Without it, the human being is simply another animal in the animal kingdom. The animal kingdom is rich in creativity, resourcefulness, and intelligence itself. However, there is no other creature with the mental capabilities of human beings.

Other creatures show intelligence. For instance, more than once I was awed by the birds in my area showing up at the bird feeder. I sometimes would forget to replenish it. The birds would disappear. Yet, within minutes of being refilled, birds of different species would begin showing up.

If they had been flying in regularly to check up on the availability of food, that would be one thing. Sooner or later, the food would be there. The checking up on the feeders in mass didn't happen. They stopped coming when there was no food. They started coming when there was food. Could it be that they communicated among the species? One bird would come in. And in essence within minutes other birds would show up.

Squirrels also would frustrate me at the bird feeders. I have Ph.D. and couldn't stop the squirrels from raiding the bird feeders. I finally had to resort to bird feeders that were designed to keep squirrels from raiding the feeders. Even then, I caught squirrels hanging on with their back feet and stretching as far down the front of the feeders as they could get. They would still be able to reach a few seeds doing that. And they would hang there as long as necessary even though ample seed had fallen to the ground. They found a way to beat my squirrel proof bird feeders. And they seemed to enjoy the challenge more than the easy access to seeds which fell to the ground.

The other day, one of our cats meowed at the front door. I thought it wanted in. On hearing that meow another one of our cats ears burked up and it began moving towards the door. So I got up to let one cat in and the other out.

I was half correct. The cat outside had brought up a small lizard. When I opened the door it moved away from the door instead of coming in. The other went out in a hunting style body language.

I saved the lizard on seeing it. The cats though kept looking for it. One cat communicated with the other.

Thus, since there is a directional creative resourceful tendency which exists in animal and plant life, there is something unique about the human being. I prefer to call that uniqueness a self. So I have chosen to distinguish self-actualization as a specialized version of the actualization tendency that makes it possible to be a human being.

Self-actualization shares a great deal with the other creatures. From a physiological stand point we share a great many physical characteristics with apes. The characteristics differ in accents. For instance the brain size is different. The amount of body hair is different. The shapes of the bones are different. And naturally the DNA is different in arrangement. It is possible to take the DNA of a human being, compare it with a gorilla, and determine if the DNA came from the human or the gorilla.

What is tremendously different is the ability to think, and reason and find ways to adapt to different environments. Gorillas will not and have not found ways to get into outer-space, live at the poles, or explore the depths of the seas. Further, human language is far more complex and varied than the communication sounds of the gorilla. Therefore, a few small sections of the brain essentially are the storehouse of the processes that make a self.

Rogers (1951) wrote, "a portion of the total private world becomes recognized as 'me,' 'I,' 'myself'" (p. 497). In this he asked, "Is social interaction necessary in order for a self to develop? Would the hypothetical person reared alone upon a desert island have a self?" (p. 497).

I supply this answer. The human creature is capable of interacting with other species. Thus, the uniqueness of the human being remains even if that human being was the last one on earth. In the past year or so, a young woman was found (Half-animal, 2007), I believe in Southeast Asia, who had been lost in the jungle from childhood. She could not speak though she had learned language as a child. She apparently had adopted some behaviors of other animals that enabled her to survive. There was no doubt though that she was human.

To the second above question, I would answer, yes. She had a self, or was a self. She was simply, for a time, different than those of us who had formal human social settings. To date, I have seen no follow-up story concerning the woman's adjustment to society.

I add to the above simple description of the self that I speak of my hand, my family, my neighborhood, my job, my country, my world. When something occurs in these, I am impacted. The disasters of 9/11 had an impact on me. When I had surgery to remove my prostate, I was significantly impacted by that experience which fortunately to date worked out well in the long term.

My point is that the "self" is bigger than the brain functions or other immediate contributing factors of my body. It incorporates something of the world around it and probably often at an unconscious level. Awareness probably remains the most obvious factor in impacting the self, but I often wonder about factors outside our conscious grasp affecting us. Such factors may include the sun rising, a tidal wave in the south Pacific, or an explosion in Baghdad.

More immediately, it is doubtful that we even remember all the experiences that impact us directly on a day to day basis. These experiences help shape us, though probably aren't completely deterministic.

An aspect of the self is creativity and resourcefulness which helps the person to make decisions and have a personal say in how he or she experiences the experiences.

What is a self? The self primarily to me is my conscious self awareness. It is my thoughts, feelings and experiences.

However, my arm, heart, brain, etc., is a significant part of me. Thus, my self is also my physical, social, and spiritual domains.

In short, the self, is all that one is that makes one distinctly human.

References

Bozarth, J. (1998). *Person-centered therapy: A revolutionary paradigm*. Ross-on-Wye: PCCS Books.

Catherine, J. (2007). *Turning problems into play*. The Think Big Revolution, mp3 recording. www.thinkbigrevolution.com/files/TBR-Apr1607.mp3

Jackson, G., E. (1981). *Pastoral care and process theology*. Washington, D.C.: University Press of America.

Meador, B. D., & Rogers, C. R. (1984) Person-centered therapy. In R. Corsini (Ed.), *Current psychotherapies* (3rd., pp. 142-195). Itasca, Illinois: F. E. Peacock Publishers.

Rogers, C. R. (1951). *Client-centered therapy*. Boston: Houghton Mifflin Company

Rogers, C. R. (1980). *On becoming a person*. Boston: Houghton Mifflin Company.

'Half-animal' woman is discovered after spending 19 years alone in Cambodian jungle. (2007, January 19). FoxNews.com http://www.foxnews.com/story/0,2933,244440,00.html

Whitehead, A. N. (1978). *Process and reality*. D. R. Griffin & D. W. Sherburne (Eds.). New York: The Free Press.

Regarding Change

During a dialogue on the cct/pca network, I received the following comments (Rice 2007): "You assert that cct/pca is in some way all about openness to change. Again, I see nothing in the theory of client centered therapy to indicate that that is true. That theory posits six conditions as necessary and sufficient for positive therapeutic growth in clients. I am quite interested in discovering from where the 'openness to change' in the theory you are talking about comes. I hope that cct practitioners and, for that matter, all persons, are and remain open to positive changes in our lives. But I see no reason to jump from that hope to the conclusion that cct/pca is a theory without discernible content or shape."

At the time it did not stir a response from me, but has occurred to me since then that the issue remains.

First, the approach is about openness to client change and belief that change can and does take place

Second, my position on change is also about the evolution of the cc/pc theory.

Openness to Client Change

As an issue in relationship to clients, I have long believed and asserted that cc/pc is about facilitating change using the necessary and sufficient conditions. This change is not a formulated change whereby the therapist has some preconceived idea about how the client should change or will change. Rather, it is an assertion that change actually occurs. "Therapy is not a matter of doing something to the individual, or of inducing him to do something about himself. It is instead a matter of freeing him for normal growth and development, or removing obstacles so that he can again move forward"(Rogers, 1942, p. 29).

Actualization as Constant Change

To assert this, I need to briefly revisit the notion of self-actualization. Rogers (1980) stated: "Individuals have within themselves vast resources for self-understanding and for altering their self-concepts, basic attitudes, and self-directed behavior" (p. 115). The word "change" does not appear in that statement. Certainly, it is implied in the word "altering" and the term "self-directive." There can be no altering or self-direction if self-actualization is not about change.

Change then is basic to the approach. "The premise of the actualization tendency manifests itself as the therapist approaches the client as if the client is the only natural authority on his or her life and on the direction and process of change" (Bozarth, & Brodley, 1986, p. 267).

Lietaer (1990) wrote, "The core of the client-centered approach remains constructive personality change and how to facilitate it as a therapist" (p. 33). The focus though is not on the therapist determining what the change will or should be, but in being open to the change process naturally inherent within the client. It simply is expected that change will occur.

However, it certainly may be asserted that the therapist by virtue of offering certain conditions facilitates whatever change does occur.

"Most client-centered therapists no longer feel uneasy when defining their work as an active influencing process in which they try to stimulate the unfolding of the client's experiencing process through task-oriented interventions. As 'process experts' they have found a way to intervene actively without falling into manipulation of authoritarian control" (p. 33).

I tend to be wary of the use of the word "most" in relationship to any claim. I doubt the Lietaer actually had the occasion to discover what "most" client-centered theorists and practitioners believed.

If those task-oriented interventions are the necessary and sufficient or "core" conditions (empathy, acceptance, and genuineness), then I concur. However, Lietaer didn't appear to offer specific tasks as do other orientations like Gestalt. I suspect that, in the context of client-centered or person-centered theory and practice, he did indeed mean the traditional conditions (Rogers, 1957).

Open to Whatever Direction the Client Takes

I suppose that if one holds that self-actualization is an ongoing process then change is constant. Being open to that change might seem presumptuous as if change is somehow dependent on being open to the change.

Yet, I have seen a lot of people in counseling and psychotherapy who felt hindered and maybe even prevented from changing. "I'm stuck," is a common theme among clients.

It might be helpful to contrast what Rogers asserted as he saw it in relationship to what other orientations asserted.

"Seeing the human organism as essentially positive in nature – is profoundly radical. It flies in the face of traditional psychoanalysis, runs counter to the Christian tradition, and is opposed to the philosophy of most institutions, including our educational institutions. In psychoanalytic theory our core is seen as untamed, wild, destructive. In Christian theology we are 'conceived in sin,' and evil by nature. In our institutions the individual is seen as untrustworthy. Persons must be guided, corrected, disciplined, punished, so that they will not follow the pathway set by their nature" (Rogers, 1986, p. 127).

At the heart of hindering or preventing change is a belief that people are untrustworthy. This hindrance may actually occur because the helper is attempting to push a person in the "right" direction.

Yet, I have seen a lot of different souls in counseling and psychotherapy who felt hindered and maybe even prevented from changing. "I'm stuck," is a common theme among clients.

The person-centered approach holds that, because there is an actualization tendency, people will move in positive directions (change) in an environment rich in certain conditions. In this environment "the person is free to choose any direction, but actually selects positive and constructive pathways. I can only explain this in terms of a directional tendency inherent in the human organism – a tendency to grow, to develop, to realize its full potential" (p. 127).

I respond to this positive direction statement by saying I long felt that clients moved in negative directions as they became open to their experiences. By negative directions I mean getting more in touch with anger, or craziness, or grief, or whatever. When they were free to deal with these in therapy, I observed they then found the freedom to move out of those negative places. They didn't like those experiences, but not because I as a therapist thought they shouldn't have negative experiences. Thus I have felt this openness to move in any direction and really meaning it, facilitated movement or change in directions more suitable to the client. Furthermore, I would assert that this meant becoming more congruent with the society around the person. Yet, as I think about it, the movement also produced assertive behavior that ran contrary to some society expectations. An example could be a woman deciding to give her baby a certain name even though relatives attempt to pressure her to use a different name.

Of course, this openness to change is also worthless if there is no change to witness. In addition, as some have held, the only thing that remains constant is change.

Therapy as Restructuring of the Self

Of some interest in therapy is the difference between counseling and therapy. I have a simplistic view of the difference. I once saw counseling as dealing with the every day problems that people have: anxiety, mild depression, poor relationships, etc. Moreover, I saw therapy as in depth investigation of problems.

I changed my mind. My concepts are still simplistic. I now see counseling as the skills, attitudes, or techniques applied to client situations. In the case of the cc/ pc approach, counseling is the utilization of the core conditions.

I now see therapy as the restructuring of the self. This restructuring tradition was seen in (Rogers, 1961).

1) The client "begins to drop . . . false fronts" (p. 109).

2) The client becomes more open to "the experience of feeling" (p. 111).

3) The client makes "the discovery of self in experience" (p. 113).

4) The client develops more "trust in one's organism" (p. 118).

5) The client moves away from external locus of evaluation to "an internal locus of evaluation" (p. 119)

6) The client has a "willingness to be a process" (p. 122) rather than being a "product" reaching some end point.

Whitehead and Change

Obviously dealing with A. N. Whitehead (1978) is not directly dealing with the person-centered approach. However, Rogers was a well read person and explored what others had to say which helped him articulate the approach. It has occurred to me that speaking of the approach using another framework is valuable.

However, the following material is so simple that it doesn't come close to dealing with the complexity of Whitehead. I see this as an effort to illustrate my point about change and insert it. One should read Whitehead to get the ultimate feel for Whitehead.

In Whitehead, a very basic premise is the "occasion." This as best I can describe it is a moment of experiencing. "Each moment of experiencing . . . has an identical structure. It begins in the initial phase, grows together through intermediate or supplemental phases, and completes itself in the final phase or 'satisfaction'" (Jackson, 1981, pp. 3-4).

There is an assumption of a "nascent" initial phase beginning infinite possibilities emerging for and from those that followed and continuing to operate. When an occasion reaches satisfaction, it "passes into immortality" (p. 24). It is "grasped" or "prehended" in the initial phase of the following occasion. Of course, in the present, there are uncountable occasions occurring all the time.

These potentially have direct or indirect impact on successors. An occasion that has reached satisfaction has an influence on many others, some more profoundly than others. It might be similar to Jupiter having an impact on the tides of the ocean of the earth. That impact is not as profound as the impact of the moon on the earth's tides even though the moon is smaller than Jupiter. By virtue of the moon's proximity to earth, its impact is greater. Jupiter probably has no measurable impact on a planet in a solar system that is thousands of light years away.

The new occasion grasps something of the previous occasion. This also means some of the many occasions that occur just before the new occasion manifests itself are grasped by the new occasion.

However, the new occasion puts its own unique twists to the experience. The image of snow flakes in part comes to mind. There is a basic structure to all snowflakes. However, it has long been asserted that no two snowflakes are exactly alike.

It is inherent in the occasion then to both conform to the past and to be creative with the new moment. Thus change is constantly occurring even while the same structure may be evident.

For Whitehead, the occasion has within it the nature to move toward novelties. The occasion's ability to add a novel twist to itself makes it unique. It differs from its predecessors while at the same time incredibly similar to its predecessors.

In short, change and similarity go hand in hand.

The Evolution (Change) of the Approach

Part of the issue that was addressed by the material in the post I received above was that I have asserted that the approach would change and has changed. Charges of misunderstandings and distortions have long been asserted (Bozarth, 1995, & 1998). Eugene Gendlin's "Focusing" stirred controversy. Others including Fierman (2006) assert that Kaiser is so similar to Rogers that he might be considered person-centered though not a Rogerian.

I personally can't imagine that as new people embrace the approach that they will not put their own twists to understanding and interpreting it. (Lietaer, 1990) affirmed differing perspectives and their legitimacy. "In my opinion, the diversity and divergence should be applauded. It is part of the richness of our approach, and is in fact the logical consequence of the client-centered basic philosophy, i.e. not to submit slavishly to authority but to seek one's own way in a personal and experiential manner. Rogers always tried to oppose doctrinarianism and dogmatism" (pp. 21-22).

I simply can't grasp why people would resist the changes so adamantly with charges of misinterpretation and distortion.

Whitehead (above) long ago claimed that change is occurring all the time. He developed a very complex theory that attempting in part to explain how change takes place. Why does it appear that some are seemingly surprised and resistant to the change?

In my own pilgrimage whereby I now question such concepts as unconditional positive regard, nonjudgmentalness, and nondirectiveness, I have been accused in community meetings of trying to start a new theory. I have been told that is fine if that is what I want to do, but to stop calling what I present as being person-centered. Fortunately, there is no governing body that can make me, or anyone, do that. Furthermore, to back down from my questions would be to essentially succumb to pressure to either conform or get out of claiming I am person-centered.

Experiential and Cognitive Relativism

For years I misused the word "phenomenological" as the word to describe the notion that people have a variety of perspectives. By definition the word is better used to describe the study the object of awareness. There is perhaps an implication of a variety of perspectives, but I do not now see that it is overt.

I have decided that a combination of experiential and cognitive relativism would be better suited. Moreover, with that I may have bitten off more than I can chew. Basically, I am asserting that the person-centered approach has long held that people bring different perspectives into therapy. That is because being different individuals people have a incredible array of experiences that impact their development. Even twins (Cardon, Fulker, DeFries, & Plomin, 1992; Emde, Plomin, Robinson, Reznick, Campos, Corley, DeFries, Fulker,

Kagan, & Zahn-Waxler, 1992) growing up in the same environment turn out differently.

My position on this might be captured very well in the tradition illustration of "The Blind Men and the Elephant" (John Godfrey Saxe)

"It was six men of Hindustan
To learning much inclined,
Who went to see the Elephant
(Though all of them were blind)
That each by observation
Might satisfy the mind.

The first approached the Elephant
And happening to fall
Against his broad and sturdy side
At once began to bawl:
"Bless me, it seems the Elephant
Is very like a wall".

The second, feeling of his tusk,
Cried, "Ho! What have we here
So very round and smooth and sharp?
To me 'tis mighty clear
This wonder of an Elephant
Is very like a spear".

The third approached the animal,
And happening to take
The squirming trunk within his hands,
Then boldly up and spake:
"I see," quoth he, "the Elephant
Is very like a snake."

The fourth reached out an eager hand,
And felt about the knee.
"What most this wondrous beast is like

Is mighty plain," quoth he;
"'Tis clear enough the Elephant
Is very like a tree!"

The fifth, who chanced to touch the ear,
Said: "E'en the blindest man
Can tell what this resembles most;
Deny the fact who can,
This marvel of an Elephant
Is very like a fan!"

The sixth no sooner had begun
About the beast to grope,
Than, seizing on the swinging tail
That fell within his scope,
"I see," quoth he, "the Elephant
Is very like a rope!"

And so these men of Hindustan
Disputed loud and long,
Each in his own opinion
Exceeding stiff and strong,
Though each was partly in the right
And all were in the wrong.

So oft in theologic wars,
The disputants, I ween,
Rail on in utter ignorance
Of what each other mean,
And prate about an Elephant
Not one of them has seen!"

In the person-centered approach, the therapist is interested in these different perspectives and hopefully attempts to get at them without ranting and raving at the differences.

If it is true that there is essentially a snowflake effect, people are similar but the same. It seems to me that these differences, however minute, would have in impact on the theory itself. The minute differences in interpretation would add up.

However, we cannot possibly speak of minute differences of perspectives among unrelated people of a society. A much wider spectrum of beliefs, experiences, ideals, thoughts, and ideas would come into play.

If indeed this approach does not force people to conform or at least doesn't claim to, then even using the presuppositions of the Process Theory of A. N. Whitehead, we would expect change to occur in the theory because of the introduction of different perspectives and differences in grasping ideas.

I assert there has been. From Rogers, to Gendlin, to Wexler & Rice, to Bozarth, to Lietaer, to Bower, there are differences of interpretation. I assert that there are as many changes in the approach as there are individuals.

If the approach respects the variety of perspectives of the clients and people it engages as facilitators, it should also be respectful of the changes within its own domain. I thus hold a similar position to Lietaer above. Our diversity is exciting, not a threat. Charges of misunderstanding and misrepresentation fail to indicate an effort to be empathic with those who engage the approach but talk about it differently than those who preceded them.

I am in favor of celebrating the diversity. It represents change and opportunities for new directions.

References

Bozarth, J. D. (1995). Person-centered therapy: A misunderstood paradigmatic difference? *The Person-Centered Journal*, 2(2), 12-17.

Bozarth, J. D. (1998). *Person-centered therapy: A revolutionary paradigm*. Ross-on-Wye: PCCS Books.

Bozarth, J. D., & Brodley, B. T. (1987). Client-centered psychotherapy: A statement. *Person-centered Review*, 1(3), 262-271.

Cardon, L. R., Fulker, D. W., DeFries, J. C., & Plomin, R. (1992). Continuity and change in general cognitive ability from 1 to 7 years of age. *Developmental Psychology*, 28, 64-73.

Emde, R. N., Plomin, R., Robinson, J., Reznick, J. S., Campos, J., Corley, R., DeFries, J. C., Fulker, D. W., Kagan, J., & Zahn-Waxler, C. (1992). Temperament, emotion, and cognition at 14 months: The MacArthur longitudinal twin study. *Child Development*, 63, 1437-1455.

Fierman, L. B. (2006). *Shrink*. Nevada City, CA: Blue Dolphin.

Jackson, G. E. (1981). *Pastoral care and process theology*. Washington D.C.: University Press of America.

Lietaer, G. (1990). The client-centered approach after the Wisconsin Project: A personal view on its evolution. In G. Lietaer, J. Rombauts, & R. Van Balen (Eds.). *Client-centered and experiential psychotherapy in the nineties*. Leuven, Belgium: Leuven University Press, 19-45.

Rice, B. (E-mail communication, July 14, 2007)

Rogers, C. R. (1942). *Counseling and psychotherapy*. Boston: Houghton Mifflin Company.

Rogers, C. R. (1957). The necessary and sufficient conditions of therapeutic personality change. *Journal of Consulting Psychology*, 21, 98.

Rogers, C. R. (1961). *On becoming a person*. Boston: Houghton Mifflin Company

Rogers, C. R. (1986). Rogers, Kohut, and Erickson: A personal perspective on some similarities and differences. *The Person-Centered Review*, 1(2), 125-140.

Saxe, J. G. (2007). *The blindmen and the elephant.* http://en.wikisource.org/wiki/The_Blindmen_and_the_Elephant

Whitehead, A. N. (1978). *Process and reality.* New York: The Free Press

Power Stuff

I never saw "The Hunchback of Notre Dame" from beginning to end. One evening I discovered Charles Laughton's 1934 interpretation of Quasimodo. I didn't realize that it was also one of Maureen O'Hara's first roles. So there was an extra treat.

The story line reeked of oppressive, manipulative, controlling power issues. Brutality, bigotry, and meanness abound. Quasimodo was on one hand rescued from his fate of severe deformity, while he was hidden away in the sanctuary of the Church. When he made the mistake of looking upon Esmeralda, he was impacted by the power of her beauty and quickly humiliated by the crowd.

Yet, on the other hand, in Quasimodo's lowly state, it is Quasimodo who aided Esmeralda after she was framed for the murder of Phoebus. Sentenced to her death, Quasimodo rescues her and uses the power of the sanctuary of the Church, and the isolation of the bell towers to protect Esmeralda.

These fail, but the ensuing conflict results in Esmeralda's freedom.

Quasimodo thought is left with a broken heart as Esmeralda joins Gringoire (played by Edmond O'Brian, another delightful treat for me) as they head off romantically through the town square.

At every turn power issues appear throughout the film.

The issue of the use or misuse of power has plagued human kind throughout history. We are not immune to it today.

It can be asserted that the person-centered approach offers an alternative to authoritarian power in the form of personal power.

This chapter will present material on power-plays in the extreme.

It will also assert that indeed the approach is set up to facilitate the use of person power to liberate self, and others to be full participants in human interactions and social behaviors like politics. It is not about pulling power-plays on others.

In the Extreme - The Abuse of Power

I don't remember when I first discovered Victor Frankl's (1963) book "Man's Search for Meaning." I thought I was picking up a psychological treatise regarding the search for meaning. And I did. However, it was nothing like I had expected.

I have a love hate relationship with reading. I like to push into new arenas and discover new worlds and perspectives. However, my attention span is short, and after a few minutes of reading, I lose my focus and desire. I keep pushing myself and make it through almost all the book projects I tackle. The only books I don't make it through are the one's I find disappointing in some way.

Little did I know that Frankl's work would become the only book that I would ever read that I could not put down. In fact, the only times I stopped reading it was when I had other responsibilities to which to tend. I finished it quickly. Quickly for me is a couple of days. My step-father Russell would read a whole book in less than I day.

In typical fashion, I highlighted material as I read in hopes of finding it quickly when I needed to. And such is the case of Frankl's work. Unfortunately, I have a host of books that I did that to and have hardly ever revisited them to hone in on that highlighted material.

For those who are familiar with Frankl's work, "Man's Search for Meaning" is an obvious personal reflection on the horrors of the extremes of the misuse of power. For those who are not familiar with it, it is Frankl's "inside story of a concentration camp, by one of its survivors." In this, it does not focus on recounting horror stories as much as it reflects on what I am going to call "attitudes."

I am using this work to point to the extreme in power abuse. For those familiar with the atrocities of Nazi Germany and the concentration camps, the example below will speak volumes beyond

Frankl's words. Yet, I fear that maybe too many people are no longer encountering even the history of those years that even we "Baby Boomers" did. Obviously, the "Baby Boomers" didn't have to deal directly with Nazi Germany. With the deteriorating awareness of those years and events, there are those who may not be able to fill in the horrors surrounding Frankl's description.

I assert the extreme of power abuse is captured in these brief words from Frankl:

"We were told to leave our luggage in the train and to fall into two lines – women on one side, mean on the other – in order to file past a senior SS officer. Surprisingly enough, I had the courage to hide my haversack under my coat. My line filed past the officer, man by man. I realized that it would be dangerous if the officer spotted my bag. He would at least knock me down; I knew that from previous experience. Instinctively, I straightened on approaching the officer, so that he would not notice my heave load. Then I was face to face with him. He was a tall man who looked slim and fit in his spotless uniform. What a contrast to us, who were untidy and grimy after our long journey! He had assumed an attitude of careless ease, supporting his right elbow with his left hand. His right hand was lifted, and with the forefinger of that hand he pointed very leisurely to the right or to the left. None of us had the slightest idea of the sinister meaning behind that little movement of a man's finger, pointing now to the right and not to the left, but far more frequently to the left.

It was my turn. Somebody whispered to me that to be sent to the right side would mean work, the way to the left being for the sick and those incapable of work, who would be sent to a special camp. I just waited for things to make their course, the first of many such times to come . . .

The significance of the finger game was explained to us in the evening. It was the first selection, the first verdict made on our existence or non-existence. For the great majority of our transport, about 90 percent, it meant death" (pp. 16-18).

There are Lesser Extremes in Daily Life

Gestalt therapy (Perls, 1975) presents a characterization called "Top Dog." "Top Dog can be described as righteous, bullying, punishing, authoritarian, and primitive" (p. 76). In one sense, this characterization is about an inner battle that one has with one's self. But in another sense, it reflects an outer reality of power-plays in relationship to what Perls called "Under Dog." Under Dog (Simkin, 1975) says in this relationship, "I'm going to do better next time, I promise" (p. 10). It is a position of submission.

A number of years ago, I began associating with a local high school baseball team. I had been involved with the football program for a number of years.

After three or four years, the head coach took a new position in another high school. An assistant coach took over the program. I was asked to go with the former head coach, but declined calling on my support of the athletes.

Into the summer ball season I witnessed what I regarded as one of the most atrocious acts of controlling, bullying, and punishment I had ever seen in sports.

I was with the eighth grade team following a double header with a neighboring school. They were out-gunned (so to speak). An older team showed up. They were more mature physically and more experienced.

In the first game, the visiting team was soundly ahead, but in the last inning, our team started performing well. When it was all finished, we lost by one run. It was a great finish though it fell short.

But in the second game, it was a blow-out. Our players made so many mistakes, mainly from the new players, that some came into the dugout with tears in the eyes. The game was ended on a "Mercy Rule."

The new head coach, who was not coaching the team, since an assistant was, came out the stands. He began running the players, using wind sprints called "baggers." With each wind sprint, he scolded and berated the players for their poor performances.

Initially, I watched as this is not an uncommon practice among coaches. But this time the coach didn't stop. His push for wind sprints continued. It became excessive. Athletes were beginning to double up in pain. Some were pleading for the coach to stop. A couple of players fell to their knees. A couple others were crying in their pain.

I got caught in the "Under Dog" role myself and assumed a helpless role of watching.

I finally had enough and left dismayed with myself for not saying anything. I was angry in what I witnessed. But when I put my equipment back in my van, I returned. The wind sprints were continuing. I couldn't believe my eyes.

With one last jog to the foul pole, the coach assembled the team.

I was so furious, I distanced myself, and paced back and forth while I waited for the coach to finish. His scolding went on and on, but I was so too far away to hear the specific words. I was restless in my anticipation of sharing my feelings with the coach.

Parents were standing frozen in place. I found out later they were overwhelmed.

Finally, the coach finished. He came up to me and said, "We are going to turn this program around."

I said, "I hope so."

I added, "But that was one of the most vicious, brutal and mean spirited displays of coaching I have ever witnessed."

Naturally, the coach was taken aback and began to defend his position. My intensity and conviction did not subside with his explanations.

He was furious. I was furious.

The next day, I visited the athletic director and shared my observations and said, if the coach's behavior continued there is going to be a major problem for the school. I couldn't imagine parents or athletes tolerating such behavior.

The coach changed his behavior until the last game of the varsity's summer schedule when they lost a double header to a visiting team.

He repeated the same behavior.

I walked off the field. I complained again with the athletic director who dismissed my complaint. I later filed an official complaint with the principal.

I was asked just before baseball season the following spring by the athletic director not to volunteer with the program. So I joined the former head coach at his new program.

My former team under the abuse of power only won 2 games. Athletes were hurt emotionally and discouraged. They were constantly belittled and criticized. Several told me they won their two games after the coach gave up and resigned to accept another job. He told them to play their game, and when they did, they won two out of the last four.

The coach is no longer with the program. He never admitted he was overly heavy handed. He felt that he had been victimized by parents, athletes, and supporters.

This problem is not an uncommon problem with youth athletics. Umpires, fans, athletes, and coaches are psychologically, and all too often physically beat-up on when things go wrong on a chronic basis during competition. And all too often coaches, parents, and fellow athletes are brutal in their behavior towards their own team mates.

It illustrates abuse of power.

At a less intense level, shortly after I was ordained, I was called the office of my District Superintendent for rumors of being a homosexual. The United Methodist Church has a statement on this issue. Homosexuality is seen as incompatible with the Christian faith. So is divorce for that matter.

I had invited a friend of mine, who needed a place to stay, to rent a room in the parsonage. I cleared it with the Church. He attended worship every Sunday. His room was upstairs. Mine downstairs.

Somehow rumors started circulating. In hearing a rumor, the D.S. called me to his office. There in rests the power-play. He called me to his office. He could have called me. He could have come see me. He could have pulled me aside at a ministers' meeting for clarification. But I had to go to his office to defend myself. The key to the power-play was having to defend myself.

On my explanation, he was satisfied. It is a minor incident. And people are called to the office of supervisors frequently in employment situations. It is almost taken for granted. And some may not even view it as a power-play.

My friend moved out a few months later never knowing about the rumor. And a year later, I was married.

There was a more annoying incident 3 or 4 years later. Again, I was called into the D.S. office. I was in a new district in a full time church. The Church had a history of falling short of its obligations to pay apportionments. Apportionments are funds that are levied to the local Church to enable the Annual Conference, and the United Methodist Church to carry out its ministries.

I got the Church to pay its apportionments, but the Church was not sending extra money for other Methodist missions and ministries.

Taking note of this, the District Superintendent called me into his office. He scolded me for not getting money to other projects.

We had made great strives towards getting apportionments paid. The scolding was uncalled for and condescending. Further, it didn't change anything. It was simply an act of bullying.

Focusing on political power, though in a generic sense, Rogers (1977) wrote:

> "Politics in the present-day psychological and social usage, has to do with *power and control*: with the extent to which persons desire, attempt to obtain, possess, share, or surrender power and control over others and/or themselves. It has to do with the maneuvers, the strategies and tactics, witting and unwitting, by which such power and control over one's own life and others' lives is sought and gained – or shared or relinquished. It has to do with the locus of decision-making power: who makes the decisions which, consciously or unconsciously, regulate or control the thoughts, feelings, or behavior of others or oneself. It has to do with the effects of these decisions and these strategies, whether proceeding from an individual or a group, whether aimed at gaining or relinquishing control upon the person himself, upon others, and upon the various systems of society and its institutions" (pp. 4-5).

Rogers expressed concern about "directive" models exuding power over clients by use of diagnosis, evaluation, care-plans, analysis, and treatment all being under the auspices of the psychotherapist. He shunned the "therapist knows best" aspect of the directive models.

Personal Power

Part of me wants to think that the person-centered approach offers a different paradigm regarding the use of power. However, part of me is uncertain about that.

When I first connected to the person-centered workshop at Warm Springs in 1987, I was excited. I was going to get a chance to meet person-centered adherents from around the country. I felt I made connections with the participants that I had not been able to make in other settings.

However, I took notice of my perception that there was elitism. There were those who had been placed on some pedestal even though they may not have actually sought that pedestal. They were portrayed as experts in an approach that denies it practitioners are experts for others (Bozarth, 1998).

Considering the notion of equality, nondirectiveness, and the rejection of the therapist as expert model espoused by the approach, some of us who saw this were disappointed.

There were those who were perceived as being "experts" in the field. Many I have used as reference material myself. Thus, the approach really hasn't gotten away from the "expert" model.

However, these "experts" were not recognized as such by some formal organization. Rather, they gained their recognition by their networking, their relationships, and their academic contributions regarding the Person-Centered Approach.

This contrasts against institutional models.

Just before I prepared this section, I received several email notices from the United Methodist News Service. They announced the election of new Bishops.

In the North Georgia Conference there are rumors, wheeling and dealing concerning favorite candidates, and campaign plans (usually informal) to get certain ministers nominated.

As I grew up in the Methodist Church, I had naively thought it was about character. And it is, but I was ignorant of the behind the scene interactions. I suspect that these interactions would appear to be similar to the old smoke-filled room politics of political parties.

This doesn't happen in the person-centered approach. There is no institutional hierarchy made of individuals who are locked into the institution.

The pecking order stuff doesn't seem to exist in the formal sense. However, I am convinced it does exist in the informal sense.

The New Model?

Shunning the Role of Expert

A long held position of the Person-Centered Approach (Rogers, 1940) as been its assertion that the therapist does not take on the role of expert for the client. This position became more adamant through the years. "Our educational system, our industrial and military organizations, and many other aspects of our culture take the view that the nature of the individual is such that he cannot be trusted – that he must be guided, instructed, rewarded, punished, and controlled by those who are wiser or higher in status" (Rogers, 1977, pp. 8-9).

I find myself wondering if this is also a put down of the efforts of fellow human beings to be helpful. It says our way is superior to the way of others.

And I find myself believing that, even if there are those poor helpless persons who need guidance from someone else, surely there is something of the blind leading the blind in this guidance?

At the heart of the nondirective model that Rogers' espoused is this: "'the individual has within himself vast resources for self-understanding, for altering his self-concept, his attitudes, and his self-directed behavior – and that these resources can be tapped if only a definable climate of facilitative psychological attitudes can be provided'" (p. 7).

During a time of play at a Warm Springs Person-Centered workshop, we let our hair down and had a variety show of sorts. In keeping with the approach, there were no plans. People simply participated.

I got up and shared this joke that I made up on the spot as some comedy efforts were being generated. At least, I think I made it up.

How many person-centered therapists does it take to unscrew a light bulb?

None.

The light bulb will unscrew itself.

Of course, the therapist in the approach offers the core conditions which allegedly empower the client to direct him or herself.

I have long held an appreciation for Gestalt therapy. I thought Fritz Perls was a little brash or curt when I observed him during films of his presentation. However, I have longed liked many of the ideas expressed in the therapy.

One of those ideas seems compatible with the client as expert slant of the Person-Centered Approach. Enright (1975) wrote, "The patient makes his own interpretations, formulates his own direct statements to others and achieves his own awareness. We see this not as thrusting the patient's responsibility for his own behavior onto him, but rather refusing to permit him to thrust it onto us." There is no effort to gain power over the client or direct healing or growth.

This seems consistent with Rogers (1940) position. He wrote of the approach: "It aims directly toward the greater independence and integration of the individual rather than hoping that such results will accrue if the counselor assists in solving the problem" (p. 28.).

Give Up Institutional Authority

Of particular appreciation for me has been the notion that the therapist gives up institutional authority (Bozarth, 1981). This institutional authority can be either from the local facility offering psychotherapy, or from a professional organization, or state authority. "I am Dr. Bower, you are in my office, on my furniture, dealing with my knowledge and I know better than you."

Now the above statement is rather presumptuous, but I have seen it at work through the years. Bozarth (1998) expresses concern about the issue of "knowing best." "The potency of the approach can not be fully realize if the trust of the client by the therapist is short-circuited with the interventions and with the therapist's ideas of what is 'really' best for the client" (p. 4).

I wonder in this though if the therapist is willing to trust the client with fresh ideas and slants. For Bozarth, this is a violation of trust.

I tried to incorporate the notion of giving up institutional authority in a study I was doing while I worked on a Masters degree in pastoral counseling (Bower, 1985). The languid effort was seen by my supervisors as being an expression of hostility towards the authority of the ordained person called a pastoral counselor. I actually found it liberating myself, and my review of my assertions was far too impotent to be considered hostile. I continue to deny that my assertions on giving up institutional authority are hostile.

However, I have enough of a psychoanalytic/psychodynamic slant in my background to see that someone looking at my position would see it as rejection and thus hostility. And enough to say, "Yes, you are right." I would add, "so what? If it just a position of one person does it really matter? And has not the world of theory changed because someone was hostile in some way with the status quo? And is not anger a valid feeling anyway?

And it felt good to write that.

I have to concur with Bozarth that there is power in the liberation that comes with not holding institutional power over the head of a client.

Facilitating

"Therapy is not a matter of doing something to the individual, or of inducing him to do something about himself. It is instead a matter of freeing him for normal growth and development, of removing obstacles so that he can again move forward" (Rogers 1977, p. 6).

The personal power of the person-centered therapist is not doing something to someone to cure, heal, or fix the person. By definition, "facilitate" (n.d.) means "1. to make easier or less difficult; help forward (an action, a process, etc.): Careful planning facilitates any kind of work. 2. to assist the progress of (a person)."

If the client is not fighting off the therapist's intrusion as he or she probes, analyzes and interrupts the client's true intentions, the client is less defensive. The notion of resistance is absent for the most part in person-centered literature. It is not an issue because the person-centered therapist doesn't presuppose (Bozarth, 1998) what direction the client should take, or what the client should or shouldn't talk about. The client can speak of anything, or withhold anything. I put it this way: Can I tell you whatever I feel I need to tell you? Can I withhold whatever I feel I need to withhold or will you criticize me, over analyze me, misinterpret me, or insist that I am being resistant or defensive when I keep stuff to myself?

Interestingly enough, the client actually becomes more open about those deeper experiences faster. This is not the same as healing. I am not making a claim that the outcome of Person-Centered Therapy is superior to other forms of therapy. Research doesn't support such superiority of outcomes. As I have done therapy, I simply didn't find the client's resistant because I didn't push them to get at their deeply held suppressed material. I didn't attack the defenses. When I did, I violated the approach and didn't experience success at getting to the deep stuff of the life of the client.

Also, I assert that the attitudes (core conditions) are about getting a glimpse of the client's world and experiences anyway. Thus, they are essentially windows by which to view the change that takes place. This change is constant, though not necessarily wanted by persons who are experiencing problems. It may not even be noticed by the client who is caught up with ongoing problems.

Rogers (1951) noted a movement from the client talking about his or her problems, to an increased awareness and openness to one's experiences and the experiences of others.

While Rogers and others have tended to shy away from the therapist being a part of that movement, I have just enough Alfred North Whitehead Process Philosophy to feel that the core conditions enable or empower such movement. They may even alter the world of the client is such a way that the client can have this movement.

In saying that, I don't believe the therapist makes this happen. I would be aghast at an effort to coerce clients to move in a positively perceived manner. That coercion would contradict the effort anyway and would sabotage the growth that Rogers noted.

On the other hand, I presented an effort (Bower, 2000) in which I asserted that the absence of the core conditions was significant in relationship to psychosis, violent behavior, anxiety, and other troubling behaviors that people experience. Misunderstanding, rejection, and facades bring out the worst in people and help keep people stuck in states of incongruence.

I deny though that using the core conditions forces people out of difficult positions. Rather, they promote ease in growth and change.

Via Participating

It is the participation of the therapist in the process that makes it possible. If a client could do it all by him or her self, he or she would. The therapist may be one of the few and maybe at times the only source of positive experiences for the client.

If the client has vast resources for personal growth and change, I am one of the client's resources. I offer empathy (which I am convinced is not always intellectual understanding, but includes the effort to understand), acceptance, and genuineness. I believe they make a difference.

I return to the baseball team I worked with. The first year I associated with them, the team struggled. It didn't make it into the playoffs. I had the audacity to believe I was having a positive impact on the team. I kept reinforcing belief in the players and the team. I kept participating in the dugout as a supporter.

The second and third years, the team made it into the playoffs. We won some games that we didn't think we could. We lost a couple games we probably shouldn't have. It was the first time that any team in the history of the school ever played consecutive years in the play-offs.

The following year collapsed, but there was a younger group of players who had not had their "ah-ha" experience as a team. In summer ball, they improved, but then the new coach entered into another mind set and the wheels came off. It was awful and illustrated how misunderstanding, rejection, and I had meanness bring out the worst in people.

By contrast with the new team I associated with, I brought a positive framework to plug in with others in a positive framework. I considered that framework rich in acceptance and empathy and genuineness. It was not without the absence of rejection and difficulty, but with my participation in the dugout the team had another resource for positive performance. They had the best record a team from the school had reached in recent years. They didn't make it into the playoffs as four other teams had even better records.

Three of those four teams were in the semi-finals and one won the state championship.

I inadvertently added "Oh, Yeah!" to the intensity of the dug-out. It was about participating and having an impact.

Apart from being an adult working with teenagers, I had no institutional authority. I was not employed by the school, or the school district. I simply volunteered my time. I gave away an attitude. I gave away belief in the athletes. And I gave away a willingness to hear what the athletes wanted. No one was coerced to put up with me. And no one was coerced to cooperate with me and do what I wanted. Yet, we were successful together. Each person had personal power and the team had power.

Clients and individuals seem to gain more power in relationship to others who assert their personal power rather than asserting institutional power.

References

Bozarth, J. (1981). The person-centered approach in the large community group. In G. Gazda (Ed.). *Innovations to group psychotherapy.* Springfield: Charles C. Thomas.

Bozarth, J. D. (1998). *Person-centered therapy: A revolutionary paradigm.* Ross-On-Rye: PCCS Books.

Enright, J. B. (1975). An introduction to Gestalt therapy. In F. Douglas Stephenson (Ed.), *Gestalt therapy primer.* New York: Jason Aronson.

facilitate. (n.d.). Dictionary.com Unabridged (v 1.1). Retrieved July 23, 2008, from Dictionary.com website: http://dictionary. reference.com/browse/facilitate

Frankl, V. E. (1963). *Man's search for meaning.* New York: Pocket Books.

Perls, F. S. (1975). Gestalt therapy and human potentialities. In F. Douglas Stephenson (Ed.), *Gestalt therapy primer.* New York: Jason Aronson.

Rogers, C. R. (1940). *Counseling and psychotherapy.* Boston: Houghton Mifflin.

Rogers, C. R. (1951). *Client-centered therapy.* Boston: Houghton Mifflin.

Rogers, C. R. (1977). *On personal power.* New York, New York: Dell Publishing

Simkins, J. S. (1975). An introduction to Gestalt therapy. In F. Douglas Stephenson (Ed.), *Gestalt therapy primer.* New York: Jason Aronson.

Acceptance:

The Basic Context of the Person-centered Approach
Toward an Understanding of Acceptance

This chapter presents the basic premises of the Person-Centered concept of acceptance. I qualify this opening statement by saying that this concept is presented as seen through my eyes. I probably should not assume that I can speak for Carl Rogers or the approach.

The chapter also offers my own views on acceptance, and relates them to a clinical experience. In my view, I reject the concept of unconditional positive regard and replace it with undistracted acceptance.

On Acceptance

Acceptance of the client was regarded by Rogers (1942, 1951, 1957, & 1983) as a major factor in facilitating a therapeutic or growth enhancing environment. The general word acceptance is used in this chapter to denote this attitudinal principle that Rogers has referred interchangeably as acceptance, unconditional positive regard, prizing, and warmth.

In writing about acceptance Rogers (1957) said,

> To the extent that the therapist finds himself experiencing a warm acceptance of each aspect of the client's experience as being a part of that client, he is experiencing unconditional positive regard . . . It means that there are no conditions of acceptance, no feeling of "I like you only if you are thus and

so." It means a "prizing" of the person, as Dewey used that term. It is at the opposite pole from a selective evaluating attitude - "You are bad in these ways, good in those." It involves as much a feeling of acceptance for the client's expression of negative, "bad," painful, fearful, defensive, abnormal feelings as for his expression of "good," positive, mature, confident, social feelings, as much acceptance of ways in which he is inconsistent as of ways in which he is consistent. It means a caring for the client, but not in a possessive way or in such a way as simply to satisfy the therapist's own needs. It means a caring for the client as a separate person, with permission to have his own feelings, his own experiences" (p. 98).

Rogers came to call this unconditional positive regard (1959). However, I am most impressed with the opening line which includes: **"To the extent that the therapist finds himself experiencing a warm acceptance."**

Acceptance as Warmth

If I would be asked about the essence of positive regard, I would point to Rogers (1961).

"Can I let myself experience positive attitudes toward this other person - attitudes of warmth, caring, liking, interest, respect?" (p. 52). This makes it real clear to me that positive regard is about a positive attitude.

Feelings of warmth are difficult to articulate. They are better understood by the experience of warmth itself. At best, there seems to be reasons why we say that we have warm feelings toward others. When we feel "good" about another person, we are relaxed. When we are relaxed, the blood vessels in our body dilate. There is a relatively unrestricted flow of blood to the hands and feet and other parts of the body. The hands and feet literally become warm. Perhaps this is one reason we describe our vague "positive" feelings toward another person as feelings of warmth.

In therapy this warmth is a feeling of caring for the client. It is a feeling of liking this person who has come for counseling. And it is an interest in the world and perceptions of the client.

Acceptance as Unconditional Positive Regard

Unconditional positive regard refers to the therapist's "willingness for the client to be whatever feeling is going on at that moment - confusion, resentment, fear, anger, courage, love, or pride" (Rogers, 1977, p. 10). The therapist accepts the client, and has warm feelings toward the client. The client has worth to the therapist, and the client is prized. All these attitudes are unconditional according to Rogers. Acceptance is not contingent on the client's being other than he or she already is. The therapist does not accept some of the client's feelings as being valid or appropriate while rejecting others. He or she accepts all that the client is at any given moment during their encounter.

There raises problems, however. Does the therapist accept murder? Is suicide acceptable? Is child molestation or child abuse acceptable? Is theft acceptable? Are antisocial behaviors acceptable? Can I hold in unconditional positive regard the actions of a rapist? In good conscience, I must say that I cannot. From a detached distance, that is where the offenses don't involve me personally, dealing with persons who have committed offenses may be easy. However, is that unconditional positive regard? I tend to think not.

(Browning, 1966) addressed the issue this way. "Positive regard does not entail the attitude of approval. To illuminate the concept of unconditional positive regard further, Rogers also refers to the concept of prizing -- a term borrowed from Dewey and introduced into client-centered theory by John Butler. Prizing is differentiated from the attitude of appraising. To appraise is to evaluate some of another person's experiencings as more praiseworthy, more important, more valuable, and more worthy of concern and interest than other of his experiencings" (pp. 112-113).

Browning later states "unconditional positive regard, as a refinement of the earlier concept of acceptance, is a construct descriptive of a mode of relationship that will acknowledge the client as a person of 'worth and significance.' ... The concept of acceptance or unconditional positive regard, understood as nonselective, nonevaluative, nondistorting, and full experiencing of the feelings of the other person, is thought to communicate best such a faith in the client's worth and significance as a person" (pp. 114-115).

Unconditional positive regard has never been intended to refer to approval or disapproval of specific actions, but rather to persons. I can accept the reality that a person commits child abuse or a rape or a murder. He or she may have been an object of abuse or violence as a child. This person may well have grown up subjected to an environment which misdirected his self-actualization. In no way does this force me to condone antisocial, destructive actions.

Another thought is, that I, if placed into the same world as the client, might have behaved in similar ways. "There but for the grace of God I go." Where does one cross the fine line to commit murderer, or child abuse, or a rape? Where is the fine line between having psychotic experiences and being emotionally "healthy?" The thought of destructive acts sometimes enter the minds of "healthy" individuals. I dare say that most of us at one time or another has come close to being destructive persons.

It can also be argued that the unconditionality of positive regard is related to positive regard for the potentials, and self-actualization process of the client.

Acceptance as unconditional positive regard is seen as nonjudgmental. The therapist is not a judge pronouncing a verdict or condemning the client.

"It is impossible to be accurately perceptive of another's inner world if you have formed an evaluative opinion of that person. If you doubt this statement, choose someone you know with whom you deeply disagree and who is, in your judgment, definitely wrong or mistaken. Now try to state that individual's views, beliefs, and feelings so accurately that he or she will agree that you have sensitively and correctly described his or her stance. I predict that nine times out of ten you will fail, because your judgment of the person's views creeps into your description of them" (Rogers, 1980, p. 154).

How many of us can point to situations we were in where someone had preconceived notions about us and didn't believe in us. Instead they turned to someone else because they didn't believe in us.

Acceptance is based on the basic trust: that the client can and will move in a self-directive way. This belief in the individual helps make it possible not to be possessive and judgmental.

Writing about tennis, W. Timothy Gallwey (1974) addresses the nonjudgmental attitude in terms useable for counseling:

"When asked to give up making judgments about one's game the judgmental mind usually protests, 'But if I can't hit a backhand inside the court to save my life, do you expect me to ignore my faults and pretend my game is fine?' Be clear about this: letting go of judgments does not mean ignoring errors. It simply means seeing events as they are and not adding anything to them. Nonjudgmental awareness might observe that during a certain match you hit 50 percent of your first serves into the net. It doesn't ignore the fact. It may accurately describe your serve on that day as erratic and seek to discover the causes. Judgment begins when the serve is labeled 'bad' and causes interference with one's playing . . ." (pp. 36).

Personally, I can put the word "counseling" in several places. Still, all the greatest tennis players I got to see play showed judgmental behavior. I have seen temper tantrums turn games around. Gallwey's principle helped my game, but I found that it distracted some athletes with whom I shared the principle. I still like the principle, but the nonjudgmental attitude isn't necessary for performance.

Acceptance as Dignity and Worth

The client has worth and dignity as a person. The client is special and the therapist maintains a degree of pride in this person being human. The client is held in regard though he or she may be a broken, battered and ragged person. "The primary point of importance here is the attitude held by the counselor toward the worth and the significance of the individual" (Rogers, 1951, p. 20).

Thus, the client is to be treated as a person of worth and dignity, not some scumbag.

A Hypothesis

Rogers believed that acceptance by the therapist will facilitate self-acceptance in the client. "The message comes through to the recipient that 'this other individual trusts me, thinks I'm worthwhile. Perhaps I am worth something. Perhaps I could value myself. Perhaps I could care for myself." (Rogers, 1980, pp. 152-153). "This acceptance of each fluctuating aspect of this other person makes it for him a relationship of warmth and safety, and the safety of being liked and prized as a person seems a highly important element in a helping relationship" (Rogers, 1961, p. 34).

Some Concerns

I wanted to attempt to get at the traditional understanding of upr above even though I don't believe that positive regard can be unconditional. I am pretty sure that I didn't do the concept justice in my skepticism which I present below.

One advantage of the use of the word acceptance is that it is more widely understood, less idealistic, and less controversial than a term like unconditional positive regard.

However, it is not an unusual experience for human beings to have positive regard towards others. My grandmother had this quality on a regular basis. And I doubt very seriously that many psychotherapists fail to experience positive regard for their clients/patients over a long period of time. That is to say, I suspect that all therapists have experiences of positive regard for every client though they may also have negative regard for some clients.

I say that last statement knowing that I have heard colleagues debrief about some of the patients and give negative reports about those clients/patients. They did not believe in them. They did not like to work with them, but often had to because they were in a setting that mandated who they worked with. There were no options.

The more diagnostic, assessment oriented disciplines seem to have room for working with clients that are viewed in a poor light. It actually is seen as part of the pathology of the patient that the therapist sees what is wrong with the client/patient rather than believing in the potential of client/patient to reach greater potentials. (Frierman, 1997) even asserts that is a major problem with directive approaches that viewing clients so dimly fosters dependence on the all knowing healer. The client can't help him or her self and needs the treatment of the expert.

Do these observations imply that we are not accepting the client if we anticipate destructive behavior and hope that the client can and will stop abusing people or himself or herself? If we fail to appreciate the acts of the client, are we rejecting him or her? Does acceptance involve placing the client's actions beyond criticism?

Criticism of the person-centered approach often involves these sorts of issues. Critics sometimes cite a joke (Kirschenbaum, 1979) about a client who jumps out of the therapist's window. The person-centered therapist makes no effort to stop the client. Rogers is reported to have responded, "For the last time, No! I would not let the client jump out the window."

Rogers (1951) wrote of the approach:

> "Some counselors - usually those with little specific training - have supposed that the counselor's role in carrying on nondirective counseling was merely to be passive and to adopt a laissez faire policy . . .

"This misconception of the approach has led to considerable failure in counseling - and for good reasons. In the first place, the passivity and seeming lack of interest or involvement is experienced by the client as a rejection, since indifference is in no real way the same as acceptance. In the second place, a laissez faire attitude does not in any way indicate to the client that he is regarded as a person of worth" (Rogers, 1951, p. 27).

Perhaps the most accepting, caring, prizing act would be to interfere with the client's intended suicide or murder by calling the police. Perhaps saying to the client, "I don't want you to beat your little boy any more," is a way of expressing warm regard for the client. Such a comment does not imply, "You are the scum of the earth," but rather, "I value you and your child."

In this, the concept of acceptance as unconditional positive regard has little appeal to me. First, I haven't found any criteria for determining that positive regard can be unconditional. Nor have I seen criteria for determining whether positive regard can be routinely distinguished from conditional positive regard. Yet, the claim is that unconditional positive regard is a necessary and sufficient condition (Rogers, 1975). Second, colleagues acknowledge that they don't maintain positive regard throughout all their sessions. That positive regard would stop for any other reason other than the end of the session says it is conditional to whatever thwarts it. Third, I know that I have not had positive regard for clients and still have seen change and growth when I accepted that I didn't feel warmth towards clients and accepted that clients don't always feel warmth towards me. And fourth, I have seen positive regard quickly deteriorate to negativity and judgmentalness in person-centered communities under adversity. When confronted about that deterioration, I have seen person-centered colleagues rationalize that deterioration saying that they weren't in therapy and weren't obligated to sustain or even offer unconditional positive regard.

I have had some difficulties with the latter concept myself for sometime (Bower, 1985). These concerns have increased in intensity in recent years. I have questions which would preclude my use of the term unconditional positive regard in association with genuineness and honesty.

I find acceptance incredibly important to the process of therapy. However, I am not at all satisfied with calling it unconditional positive regard.

The word "unconditional" by definition means "not limited by conditions; absolute" (Dictionary.com). Another definition reads, "Without conditions or limitations" (The American Heritage Dictionary). Thus, by definition the absence of positive regard indicates that there was a condition to the positive regard even if that condition is an issue of losing concentration. "Unconditionality: means always, regardless of circumstances with no conditions or exceptions" (Leonard, 1998, p. 259). However, the term defies the standard definition.

Concept Not Generated From Research Data

The earliest articulations of Rogerian theory did not use the term, unconditional positive regard (Rogers, 1942; 1951). The presentations on those early sources were related to initial data and findings regarding the approach. The concept he originally espoused was about acceptance, warmth, or prizing. Thus, possible researcher bias about unconditionality had not yet been introduced.

According to Rogers (1957), the term was adopted from/or by Standahl in his 1954 dissertation entitled "The Need for Positive

Regard." So obviously the term was being used prior to 1957. It seemed to fit presuppositions about accepting clients as they are, their experiences, thoughts, and behaviors. And it seemed to fit that the therapist would sustain an attitude of warmth or prizing, no matter what the client's behavior was.

Unconditional Positive Regard Excludes Other Forms of Regard

The problem was that it discarded therapists being human beings who also have negative, or neutral regard. Unconditional positive regard excludes other forms of regard as significant to therapy and virtually insists on one kind of regard, positive regard, as superior. It thus essentially forces therapists, if they wanted to call themselves Rogerians, or client-centered, to find ways to sustain positive regard for clients no matter what.

No Criteria Established

More importantly, as mentioned earlier, no criteria were established to determine the presence of unconditional positive regard. Criteria probably cannot be established to determine if the positive regard of therapists was actually unconditional. Just because a therapist has positive regard, doesn't mean that it is unconditional. It could mean that the client simply has not pushed the right buttons to trigger the negative regard of the therapist. It could mean that the therapist is putting up a facade of unconditional positive regard. It could mean that the therapist shelved negative regard while focusing on what the client was presenting of him or her self.

In developing criteria there would be too many intangibles that could influence positive regard to make it possible to determine if positive regard is unconditional in any given moment. What may be a factor in making positive regard possible for one therapist may not be for another. Or what may be a factor in preventing a therapist from experiencing positive regard may not be a factor for another.

If there have been no criteria to establish that positive regard is unconditional, the claim that unconditional positive regard is a necessary condition of the necessary and sufficient conditions for therapy is in doubt. There can be no claim that it is necessary to the process of therapy. If it cannot actually be confirmed to exist, then to assert that it a necessary ingredient to therapy is without foundation. I believe the absence of criteria undermines the claim that it is a necessary and sufficient condition to therapy. If there were no criteria for determining that positive regard was/is unconditional, how in the world could it be claimed to be necessary and sufficient for therapy?

My own search and persistent probes within the person-centered community have failed to turn up criteria for determining that positive regard could be unconditional.

In addition, two qualitative research projects I did in the 80s (Bower, 1985, 1989) did not produce the term unconditional positive regard. If upr was there, surely it would have been noticed by the observers in those studies. If it is not obvious to observers, it stirs the question about how it came to be part of the approach and labeled as necessary and sufficient for therapy.

Too Idealistic

Thus, the concept is idealistic. It becomes a goal that cannot be reached and if reached it is so rare that by virtue of being rare, positive regard is conditional. The condition might be as mundane as the therapist's willingness to sustain positive regard, or as significant as the client doing something harmful to the therapist thus triggering negative regard from the therapist.

Even if it were possible for positive regard to actually be unconditional, it raises a concern as to how much therapy would actually be done if positive regard has to be unconditional.

Assertions by therapists that they have been able to sustain unconditional positive regard for whole sessions on demand would be suspect as the claim could not be verified. It would simply be an unverifiable assertion about the nature of therapy. The best we can do is say that in this moment the therapist is experiencing positive regard.

Too Legalistic

The concept has left beginners and experienced theorists with the notion that having positive regard is a must (Okun, 1997; Sharf, 2000). It has also generated legalism whereby practitioners and theorists have accused colleagues of failing to be person-centered. There is thus an inherent pressure to reach states of unconditional positive regard. This would appear to contradict the alleged nondirective aspect of the approach. If therapists are supposed to be unconditional with their regard, then they not only pressure adherents to adopt the nondirective attitude, they pressure themselves and impose that attitude on the client as well. The client has no choice in the matter.

Further, the therapist would have to become an expert, assuming that being nondirective is the way to help the client.

My observation or claim basically denies Bozarth's (1998) assertion. "The revolutionary crux of Rogers' theory is that the therapist does not intervene and has no intention of intervening" (p. 4). I see that assumption as an intervention. The client has to deal with it or get out of the therapy.

Accuracy in Communication is Thwarted

In (Bower, 1985), I expressed concern that the therapist would get lost in the attitude of empathy and unconditional positive regard. If I am so locked into communicating positive regard in order to be congruent with conceptions of the approach, surely, I would not communicate accurately or openly my negative regard. I am convinced this holds up under casual scrutiny. The open therapist is covered-up or hidden in the effort to sustain unconditional positive regard.

Many years ago I remember a demonstration with a person-centered practitioner. The volunteer client expressed a number of sexist issues during the demonstration. Each one was met with the appearance of acceptance via empathic responses. However, in a following community meeting the person who gave the demonstration jumped all over the person for the sexist views he shared during the demonstration. The therapist had withheld those views from the volunteer client and the audience. There would have been no way to know the therapist actually felt such negativity towards the client had it not been for what occurred by coincidence in the community meeting that followed. The positive regard offered then, was conditional positive regard.

Resistance to Rejecting Unconditional Positive Regard

When I began questioning the validity and accuracy of unconditional positive regard, the subjective responses were surprising to me. I was told I failed to understand the concept. It was really just an ideal. Therapists were capable of sustaining unconditional positive regard in therapy even if they didn't practice it outside of therapy in person-centered communities. Thus, the term was limited to unverified situations called counseling or psychotherapy. Others said, they simply chose to call acceptance unconditional positive regard, and it didn't matter if it held up under scrutiny or not.

In the midst of a dialogue on the cct/pca Internet community, I got a private post from John Shlien telling me that he did not believe in unconditional positive regard, but that it was futile to attempt to address the issue in the person-centered community because it is so ingrained in it.

Another Offering on Acceptance

In my questions, my concerns, I am not abandoning acceptance. Rather, I offer an alternative term or phrase regarding acceptance. It seems reasonable to me of have an alternative for the concept of unconditional positive regard that reflects the reality, if that is possible, of acceptance rather than an ideal. After all, the claim is that the condition is necessary and sufficient for therapy. How can an idealistic claim be necessary and sufficient? So I offer the following material for consideration.

Acceptance as Undistracted Acceptance

It is real clear to me that acceptance as been determined to exist and to be significant to counseling and psychotherapy. The list of sources for this claim is extensive. I see no need to attempt to prove its importance in light of a myriad of sources available in a good library and via the Internet.

Being dissatisfied with the term unconditional positive regard I have sought another. I have found that in as much as the therapist can accept the client in all manner of situations, that the condition of acceptance is met.

So for this "in as much as" claim or what Rogers above said "to the extent that," I have coined the term "**undistracted acceptance**." I have had experiences, and witnessed it among my supervisees, whereby I accepted the client at such levels that there seemed to be nothing else going on in the world. All my focus, attention, and concentration were upon this moment with this client. They actually occur very often in my experience.

I am not prepared to say these experiences are examples of positive regard. They actually may be similar to being in a hypnotic state. They seem to have some of the same qualities: time distortion, increased awareness, high degrees of focus and concentration, even age regression, and the ability to shut out distractions while at the same time noting the existence of other phenomenon. They may also be similar to an athlete tending to certain aspects of his or her self during a game.

During these moments, the client may be speaking about killing his sister and the therapist really-really-really receives what the client is reporting. Even though any given event is hideous to the therapist, like murder, the therapist receives what the client reports about his/her experiences. And even though the therapist may believe in the death penalty for that behavior, someone else determines the legal guilt and consequences. The therapist is simply creating a therapeutic environment and is not the judge and jury.

To put it simply, the therapist is undistracted in any given moment regardless of the regard. The incident I shared above of the demonstration probably illustrates this. The person giving the demonstration was so focused on the person who volunteered as the client that she did not tend to the distractions of her negative experience. The session was about the client, not the therapist.

However, I assert that in that in any given moment the therapist may be distracted and get in touch with negative or neutral regard. I sometimes wonder if the positive regard might itself be a distraction. In undistracted acceptance there are no claims of unconditionality. If the therapist might be distracted or can be distracted if the right conditions exist, acceptance is conditional.

My assertion is that any person who so desires can reach these states of mind. And of course the desire to do so is a condition for the acceptance. It is not an idealistic state of mind. It is reachable and obtainable.

The necessary and sufficient condition of acceptance does not have to reach the level of unconditional positive regard. All that may be necessary and sufficient is acceptance of the experiences, reports, thoughts, and ideas of the client by the therapist. I actually believe that when the therapist receives the client into the therapeutic moment, that this acceptance is part of the over all condition of acceptance. Thus, I am not just claiming that acceptance has to be undistracted acceptance. I am asserting that in as much as the therapist accepts the client, a condition of therapy is created. As much as I like the term I coined, I am not locked into it being some mandated state of mind. I just simply note that this state of mind does exist in therapy and other experiences.

With that I want to push further on the issue of acceptance to the necessary and sufficient condition of what I want to call radical acceptance. In radical acceptance, it is not a matter of limiting the acceptance to positive regard. I am convinced that therapists don't have to like their clients at all to accept them. However, they do have to accept that they don't like their clients, how they feel about them, or how they view them. If they cannot do this then they have to reject the client. Also, if they fail to grasp that they don't like a particular client, they are incongruent. And Rogers (1957) asserted in his necessary and sufficient conditions, that the congruence of the therapist was one of the conditions.

Nonacceptance, however, does not equal negative regard. Turning the client away because of negative regard, beating up on clients because of negative regard, or dismissing, dominating, or degrading clients because of negative regard is nonacceptance.

However, a therapist may turn away and reject a client because of feeling positive regard for the client and feeling uncomfortable about that regard. The history of human relationships is replete with rejections between people who felt someone was getting too close. Can we expect therapists to be above that experience with clients? I think not.

Negative regard in itself is a very real and very human experience that if managed by self awareness is not dangerous to anyone. It becomes a problem when the therapist feels guilty for having negative regard, or attempts to harm the client because of that negative regard. However, simply taking note that I have experiences of negative regard and dealing openly with them is a form of acceptance. By openly, I don't mean that the therapist needs to admit the negative regard to the client. I mean that the therapist needs to be aware of having negative regard.

For instance, and I use a nontherapeutic incident here, I received a phone call from a constituent when I was a county commissioner. He was furious. He objected to a statement I made in public. He cussed me out. He yelled at me. He carried on for a long period of time. He felt miserable. I felt miserable. He didn't hold me in positive regard. And I certainly didn't hold him in positive regard. It was awful.

However, to his surprise I listened to him. And I let him know where we differed on the issue and where we agreed. I admit to feeling like hanging up on him, but I let him vent, and express himself. I can't say that either of us was nonjudgmental. We were both very judgmental.

We both finally ran out of energy. He had nothing else to say. I had no more ability to keep listening.

When I hung up the phone, my hands were shaking. I experienced anger, and anxiety, and guilt. I did not experience positive regard.

Some time later, the man came up to me and spoke to me outside of a local business that we both utilized. He received me warmly and I him. As time went on the issue he had addressed was addressed to his satisfaction. Yet, I addressed the problem on my terms, not his. He wanted to hang someone (figuratively of course), while I wanted to fix the situation. The situation he was concerned about was changed and he was satisfied and the person he was concerned about kept her job and improved her performance.

My point is, this was not about positive regard. The interaction was characterized by negative regard. It was about accepting the man's negative regard and accepting my own and then being amazed that the situation changed.

In the realm of therapy, I have provided therapy for murderers and rapists. I could say I provided therapy to people who committed murder or rape. I experienced a dim few of them as persons, thus I deliberately used the words "murderers" and "rapists." I have had very uncomfortable feelings and experiences with clients. I have even wondered if certain clients would actually even try to be better human beings. So I have to say I have experiences of negative regard in relationship with clients. But time and time again, I have still witnessed change as long as I accepted the experiences, feelings, thoughts, ideas for what they were.

I don't remember ever being mean spirited to any clients though I do know I have experienced impatience. I am not advocating that one use negative regard to be mean spirited. If the therapist is going to be mean, a referral needs to be made. I am advocating accepting the experiences, positive, negative, or neutral for what they are.

How does one do this? I believe that is where empathy comes in. When acceptance is channeled through empathy, the condition is met. This seems congruent with Bozarth's (1998) position on empathy and unconditional positive regard. I just simply reject calling warmth, prizing, and/or positive regard unconditional positive regard.

It is also where genuineness comes in. When acceptance is channeled into being open about the therapist's experience and the client's experience, the condition is met. I again qualify this; it is possible to genuinely beat up on the client. This is unacceptable and is an act of nonacceptance. In this, I default to the ethical guidelines of the helping professions. If those guidelines are transgressed by the therapist, then nonacceptance has taken place. Therapy has not occurred. Negative regard is not grounds for acting out and mistreating a client.

Acceptance as Therapy

While Brodley (1997, 1998, & 1999) appears to me to indicate the cct is linked to providing therapy only through being genuinely empathic in unconditional positive regard, I think this limits therapy. It may be in any given instant I may not understand the client, but I am accepting of the client. In any given moment I may not prize the client who is with me in therapy. However, I have come to believe that acceptance transcends the prizing. And I tend to believe that accepting the client even though I don't understand is extremely important.

As I was beginning to struggle with the concept of empathy, I started by viewing empathy as the receiving of the client into the therapist's world. As I came to see empathy as Rogers described it, the process of entering the world of the client. I needed a concept to handle the receiving of the client into the therapist's world. Acceptance is that concept. In accepting the client, the therapist opens up his or her world and receives the client into that world.

Through acceptance the client enters the world of the therapist. That is, the client is received by the therapist or the therapist cannot enter the world of the client. This is not about the client being empathic. The client is not in therapy to understand the therapist, but perhaps is in therapy to understand him or herself. The client is there to deal with his or her own problems or desires for growth (whatever growth represents for the client), and he or she is being accepted by the therapist.

Rogers asserted that a client will grow from therapy when he or she is accepted. When the therapist receives this person, the client will respond to therapy in ways relative to that particular client.

An Illustration

In my own experience as a therapist, I have found acceptance to be a valuable factor in facilitating change in a client.

I began seeing a thirty-six-year-old black woman, S, who had shot and killed her husband after years of abuse. She was tried for murder and found not guilty by reason of self-defense. However, at some point she had developed paranoid beliefs and behaviors. It was not clear whether these tendencies were already present, only to be accentuated by the tragic incident, or whether the trauma had initiated her behavior. She was suspicious that people were plotting against her. She heard voices over the intercom at work calling her to have sex with the boss. She talked about her husband as if he were a pimp. She thought that there were people who wanted to kill her because she had ruined their prostitution ring when she killed her husband. She thought that people on the street were looking at her and that they that knew she had killed her husband.

The first thing I did was to accept her, but I found it extremely difficult to enter into and understand her world. It was so garbled, chaotic, disorganized and confused that the only understanding I could manage was that it was garbled, chaotic, disorganized and confused.

However, I accepted her. While my previous non-therapy illustration reflected negative regard, this therapeutic illustration reflects positive regard. I liked her. I looked forward to seeing her. I accepted as much of the garbled content of her story as I could piece together. I accepted her view of her husband as a pimp and wondered whether he really might have been one. I accepted her feeling that people were plotting against her and I wondered if indeed someone might be plotting against her. I recalled an old saying that says, "Just because you're paranoid doesn't mean they aren't out to get you."

By the time I terminated my relationship with S, she was more coherent and easier to follow. I found that while her husband was not a pimp, he had slept with a lot of women. I verified that he had abused her. I found that people did reject S because she frightened them with behavior that they regarded as crazy and bizarre. People were afraid she would kill them as well.

In fact, in one of her more agitated states, S actually had threatened someone with a gun. On another occasion she fired a warning shot over her brother's head. There was a lot of reality in S's craziness. In fact, S's brother was attempting to find ways to take her property. She was trying to defend her interests. She just had not yet reached the level of finding more socially acceptable ways to defend her interests.

Personally, I do not believe that one hour a week of being empathic was sufficient to bring about the change which took place in this client, especially in light of the fact that initially I did not understand her world. In this case, I believe that acceptance had more power in respect to change.

Thus, I believe that my acceptance of S played an important role in facilitating change. S did not become a perfect citizen, but I believe she became a more socially functioning person. I believe with Rogers that acceptance makes a significant impact on the individual. For me, acceptance truly is one of the foundational attitudinal principles for maximizing the self-actualizing tendency.

A Word for Consideration

Before I leave this chapter, I want to reassert my claim. I do not believe that it is possible always to be accepting of the client during each moment of therapy; neither did Rogers. A footnote in his article on the "Necessary and Sufficient Conditions . . ." reveals this:

"The phrase 'unconditional positive regard' may be an unfortunate one, since it sounds like an absolute, an all or nothing dispositional concept [italicization mine for emphasis]. It is probably evident from the description that completely unconditional positive regard would never exist except in theory. From a clinical and experiential point of view I believe that the most accurate statement is that the effective therapist experiences unconditional positive regard for the client during many moments of this contact with him, yet from time to time he experiences only a conditional positive regard - and perhaps at times a negative regard, though this is not likely in effective therapy. It is in this sense that unconditional positive regard, exists as a matter of degree in any relationship" (Rogers, 1957, p. 98).

If I have a client whom I cannot accept unconditionally, if extreme bias, if hard feelings, or other factors block acceptance, I can refer the client to a colleague. Fortunately, I have yet to have this experience.

Summary:

I believe the word *acceptance* is the most appropriate word for this attitudinal principle. I have chosen it because I believe that it is broad enough to include warmth, prizing, and positive regard, with all their different connotations. I have room for the experience of negative regard in this notion of acceptance. In as much as I can accept my own negative regard and be open to it, I am also congruent enough to accept and be open to the experiences of negative regard of the client. If I am not open to that negative regard, then I need to refer the client. In this, being mean spirited, dismissive, and authoritarian are forms of acting out negative regard and have no room in client-centered/person-centered therapy. This is not acceptance.

It is the torn and broken person whom the therapist accepts. It is the person who has lost something. It is the person who appears to others to be falling apart who is accepted. Often the person coming for therapy is being rejected for not being a "together" person. The client's friends and relatives may cry, "Make him or here into something new. Make him or her better." The therapist accepts this person. To the therapist, the client is a person with tremendous capabilities as well as very real limitations.

References

Bower, D. W. (1985). Assumptions and attitudes of the Rogerian person-centered approach to counseling: Implications for pastoral counseling. Unpublished manuscript, Columbia Theological Seminary, Decatur, GA.

Bower, D. W. (1989). The attributes of five person-centered therapists. Unpublished doctoral dissertation, University of Georgia, Athens, GA.

Bozarth, J. (1998). *Person-centered therapy: A revolutionary paradigm.* Ross-on-Rye: PCCS Books.

Brodley, B. T. (1997). The nondirective attitude in client-centered therapy. *The Person-Centered Journal,* 4(1), 18-30.

Brodley, B. T. (1998). Congruence and its relation to communication in client-centered therapy. *The Person-Centered Journal,* 5(2), 83-106.

Brodley, B. T. (1999). Reasons for responses expressing the therapist's frame of reference in client-centered therapy. *The Person-Centered Journal,* 6(1), 4_27.

Browning, D. S. (1966). *Atonement and psychotherapy.* Philadelphia: The Westminster Press.

Frierman, L. B. (1997). *The therapist is the therapy.* Northvale, New Jersey: Jason Aronson,

Gallwey, W. T. (1974). *The inner game of tennis.* New York, New York: Bantom Books.

Kirschenbaum H. (1979). *On becoming Carl Rogers.* New York, New York: Delta Publishing.

Leonard, T. J. (1998). *The 28 laws of attraction: Stop chasing success and let it chase you.* New York: Scribner.

Okun, B. F. (1997). *Effective helping: Interviewing and counseling techniques.* Pacific Grove, CA: Brooks/Cole Publishing.

Rogers, C. R. (1942). *Counseling and psychotherapy.* Boston: Houghton Mifflin.

Rogers, C. R. (1951). *Client-centered therapy.* Boston: Houghton Mifflin.

Rogers, C. R. (1957). The necessary and sufficient conditions of therapeutic personality change. *Journal of Consulting Psychology,* 21. 98.

Rogers, C. R. (1961). *On becoming a person.* Boston: Houghton Mifflin Co.

Rogers, C. R. (1977). *On personal power.* New York: Delta.

Rogers, C. R. (1980). *A way of being.* Boston: Houghton Mifflin Co.

Rogers, C. R. (1983). *Freedom to learn for the 80's.* Columbus, Ohio: Charles E. Merrill Publishing.

Sharf, R. S. (2000). *Theories of psychotherapy and counseling: Concepts and cases.* Belmont, CA: Brooks/Cole.

unconditional. (n.d.). Dictionary.com Unabridged (v 1.1). Retrieved May 17, 2007, from Dictionary.com website: http://dictionary.reference.com/browse/unconditional.

unconditional. (n.d.). The American heritage® dictionary of the English language, Fourth Edition. Retrieved May 17, 2007, from Dictionary.com website: http://dictionary.reference.com/browse/unconditional.

Empathy:

A Sentient Aspect of the Approach

"If someone tells you who they are, believe them"
Maya Angelou

One day as a new driver, I was heading from Oneco, Florida to Bradenton, Florida on Highway 301. Just outside of Oneco is a divide in the road. Making a right takes one through Samoset, Florida. Making a left takes one towards Bradenton.

As I approached this intersection, which requires the drivers coming from Samoset to stop, I saw a taxi approach the stop sign. There was also traffic coming from the left fork heading south. As I watched the taxi, I said to myself, "This person is not going to stop." I put on my brakes to slow down. Sure enough, the taxi driver didn't stop and entered my lane of traffic.

I didn't have a clue as to how I knew that taxi driver wasn't going to stop. I am not prepared to argue it was some sort of mental telepathy. I suspect now that the speed of the taxi, and probably no signs that the vehicle was slowing down contributed to my believing the taxi wouldn't stop. But this happened in just an instant.

Getting at empathy is not some extra-ordinary psychic experience. It is about tending to words, gestures, voice inflections, and body languages. It simply says, as best as I can, I want to grasp what the other person is presenting.

On Basic Empathy

It is well known that Rogers (1951) wrote, ". . . it is the counselor's function to assume, in so far as he is able, the internal frame of reference of the client, to perceive the world as the client sees it, to perceive the client himself as he is seen by himself, to lay aside all perceptions from the external frame of reference while doing so, and to communicate something of the empathic understanding to the client" (p. 29). The therapist makes a commitment to perceive the internal fame of reference of the client. He/she discovers the client's experiences, joys or hurts.

Empathy occurs as an ongoing process. It takes place during an encounter between self-actualizing individuals. One person comes with experiences. These may be painful or wonderful. The therapist also comes with experiences which also may be painful or wonderful. However, the therapist is not in the therapy session to deal with his or her own experiences. They may be available in relationship to communicating with the client, but they are not available to the client for the therapist's benefit.

Engaging the World of the Client

It is empathy that gives the "client-centered/person-centered aspect to this approach. The focus is on the thoughts, experiences, and feelings of the client. The therapist seeks in this to grasp the client's perspectives. "As time has gone by we have come to put increasing stress upon the 'client centeredness' of the relationship, because it is more effective the more completely the counselor concentrates upon trying to understand the client as the client seems to himself" (Rogers, p. 420-421).

A standard definition that I have accepted essentially states that empathy is entering the world of the other person. Rogers (1961) also asked in relationship to empathy, "Can I let myself enter fully into the world of his feelings and personal meanings and see these as he does?" (p. 53).

Perhaps the phrase entering the world of the client is somewhat misleading. There is an aspect of leaving one's own world to enter the world of another. There is an aspect of giving up the therapist's world here. There are some philosophical aspects that cannot be addressed here. Is this entering even possible?

Perhaps, empathy is about perceiving the world of the client rather than entering the world of the client. An early definition represented in Rogers (1980) may capture this. "The state of empathy, or being empathic, is to perceive the internal frame of reference of another with accuracy and with the emotional components and meanings which pertain thereto as if one were the person, but without ever losing the 'as if' condition" (p. 140).

I am not sure how one can lose the "as if" part. Perhaps one can have delusions that one actually experiences the world of the other. Or perhaps, one may think that he/she is accurate in being empathic when he or she isn't. Or maybe even getting one's perspective so mixed with the perspective of the client that the therapist can't tell the difference.

Perceiving the World of the Client

If empathy is part of the heart of client-centered therapy, it is directly or indirectly related to the concept of nondirectiveness which Rogers (1980) indicated he discarded. This was apparently because of its association with "the technique of reflecting the client's feelings" or "repeating the last words the client has said" (p. 139). He (Rogers, 1980) felt that reflection and empathy became so mistakenly intertwined that he stopped writing and talking about the two for a number of years: "This tendency to focus on the therapist's responses had appalling consequences . . . The whole approach came, in a few years, to be known as a technique. 'Nondirective therapy, it was said, 'is the technique of reflecting the client's feelings.' Or an even worse caricature was simply that 'in non-directive therapy you repeat the last words the client has said.' I was so shocked by these distortions of our approach that for a number of years I said almost nothing about empathic listening" (p. 139).

Rogers (1986) restated this. "Although I am partially responsible for this use of this term to describe a certain type of therapist response, I have, over the years, become very unhappy with it" (p. 127).

Shlien (1970) wrote, "This technique was a remarkable invention, though it has been maligned by caricature and wooden application" (p. 115). I assert that reflection limited the scope of what the experience of empathy is really about. This in turn probably has stifled creative research into the range of empathic responses. Bozarth (1984) wrote "The equating of empathy with the particular technique of reflection has resulted in: (1) conceptual confusion between empathy and reflection; (2) a focus on operational methods of acting empathic; and (3) a limitation of the empathic response modes of therapists" (p. 59). It would appear to me that Bozarth in my opinion asserted that reflection as the major empathic response puts limits on empathic responses. Bozarth believes that focusing on the technique of reflection distorts the concept of empathy, such that "empathy (even by reflection) is no longer being 'able to adopt his (client's) frame of reference, to perceive with him, yet to perceive with acceptance and respect.' (Rogers, 1951, p.41)" (p. 68). Focusing on a technique distracts from being empathic in that the concentration is on the technique instead of the experience of the client.

Rogers (1980) held that empathy was far more complex than myths about it had indicated. I am laconic myself. Thus, I am sure that I don't capture the complexity of empathy in this brief chapter. I suspect a book on the topic would only limit what empathy is about as well.

A major component of the empathic process is as Rogers (1961) stated: "the therapist is experiencing an accurate, empathic understanding of the client's world as seen from the outside. To sense the client's private world as if it were your own . . . To sense the client's anger, fear, or confusion . . . When the client's world is this clear to the therapist, and he moves about in it freely, then he can both communicate his understanding of what is clearly known to the client and can also voice meanings in the client's experience of which the client is scarcely aware" (p. 284). In this phase of perceiving the client's world, it is necessary to experience understanding.

Rogers (1951) emphasizes the perceptions of the client: "It would appear that for me, as counselor, to focus my whole attention and effort upon understanding and perceiving as the client perceives and understands, is a striking operational demonstration of the belief I have in the worth and the significance of this individual client" (p. 35). The process of empathy is about perceiving the world of the client as the client shares that world. I have room for asking questions in regards to perceiving the client's world. I would like not to assume that I understand. I am sure I do make those assumptions. Questions may arise from my obviously believing that I haven't perceived what the client is presenting. They may also come of feeling muddled. Furthermore, they may occur because I am making sure that I really perceive accurately.

However, I just found myself wondering if the therapist can really only be getting in touch with his own perceptions based on what the client presents. Simply stated, if the client says, "I am angry." Can the therapist really really really understand that? Certainly, the therapist can say, "I see that you are angry." This itself is probably sufficient. However, a really deep experiential component might not really be possible for the therapist.

In this, I hope to contradict myself in a way. I attempted a number of years ago to get at how therapists know that they have grasped the client's perspective. I wasn't successful at getting at that knowing. In part, my theory on this was based on a position that if I am having feelings and experiences similar to the client's, I have a subjective confirmation of the client's experiences. Therefore, if the client is sad, and I experience sadness, I have come to believe this is a way of knowing that I have grasped a perception of the client. I make no claim in this to believe that I am experiencing the client's sadness (or other experiences). The sadness is mine. Nevertheless, I trust it tells me something about what is going on with the client.

Bozarth (1996) asserts that in the person-centered approach, there is trust that the client is the expert, the ultimate authority concerning his or her own world. (Bozarth & Brodley, 1991) and do not feel that the counselor could be the expert for the client. Thus, they reject the notion that the counselor can know what is best for the client. The traditional model of diagnosis, interpretation, analysis and the use of techniques show distrust of the client. These dismiss the client's ability to tend to and be aware of his/her own world.

Rogers (1977) wrote:

"In 1940 I began to try to change . . . the politics of therapy. Describing an emerging trend, I said, 'This newer approach differs from the older one in that it has a genuinely different goal. It aims directly toward the greater independence and integration of the individual rather than hoping such results will accrue if the counselor assists in solving the problem. The individual and not the problem is the focus. . .

Therapy is not a matter of doing something to the individual, or of inducing him to so something about himself. It is instead a matter of freeing him for normal growth and development, of removing obstacles so that he can again move forward.

I had described various counseling techniques much in use at that time - such as suggestions, advice, persuasion, and interpretation - and had pointed out that these rested on two basic assumptions: that 'the counselor knows best,' and that he can find techniques by which to move his client most efficiently to the counselor-chosen goal . . .

I had advanced the view that it was preferable simply to free the client to become an independent, self-directing person . . .

It is obvious that even this premise of client-centered therapy, without going further, has enormous political implications. Our educational system, our industrial and military organizations, and many other aspects of our culture take the view that the nature of the individual is such that he cannot be trusted - that he must be guided, instructed, rewarded, punished and controlled by those who are wiser and higher in status. To be sure, we give lip service to a democratic philosophy in which all power is vested in the people, but this philosophy is 'honored more in the breach than in the observance.' Hence simply describing the fundamental premise of client-centered therapy is to make a challenging political statement" (pp. 6-9).

The counselor's use of empathy overcomes the stance of authority over and above the client's world. At the heart of the use of empathy is trust in the client to share his/her thoughts, experiences, and perspectives. In some way, this sharing is therapeutic. It is self-directive in nature. The therapist doesn't resolve the client's situation.

Laying Aside the External Frame of Reference

To pull off empathy, the therapist has to be congruent enough, together enough, and stable enough, to set his or her stuff aside. The therapist might need to access his/her experiences during therapy to help him/her to understand or to attempt to communicate understanding. However, the therapy session is not for the therapist. Consequently, it is not an occasion for the personal growth of the therapist (though I have often felt I learned something about me from engaging clients). The process of empathy thus means putting aside all perceptions from the external frame of reference, and giving up assumptions about the client. This allows the client to speak about his or her world. It allows the therapist not to impose generalizations upon the client. In addition, it allows the therapist to hear what the client has to say about his or her own world.

This state of congruence which enables the therapist to be empathic is a position of personal power. It is not about institutional or political power. An institution such as a State or professional association may provide formal credentials. However, in the person-centered approach, the therapist functions as a person of worth and value relating to another person of worth and value. There is a commitment in this to understand the client. Assuming the role of expert, informing the client what he or she should do, or pointing out what the client doesn't know, is set aside in recognition that the client being is his or her best expert (Bozarth, 1998).

I have concerns about this extreme. There is no affirmation of the state of incongruence interfering with the client's access to the personal resources that lead to growth. It does not seem to recognize the client seeking the therapist, encountering the therapist as a resource of ideas and experiences that can possibly be used by the client. It seems to miss the therapist as a resource for options. The therapist is stereo typically reduced to unconditional positive regard and making empathic responses. Bozarth (1984) seems to want to break out of the stereotype.

In the stereotypical model, the therapist doesn't share ideas, thoughts, and experiences. These might violate the nondirective model. They could all too easily originate with the therapist in this model.

The stereotypical model position appears not to take ignorance into account. It doesn't allow for the lack of exposure to possible resolutions from outside the client, in this case the therapist.

I would ask, "Why reinvent the wheel?" If the therapist has information that potentially is helpful, it seems restrictive for the therapist to keep it to him or her self in the name of being empathic or nondirective.

I agree that "the therapist must lay aside his preoccupation with diagnosis and his diagnostic shrewdness, must discard his tendency to make professional evaluations, must cease his endeavors to formulate an accurate prognosis, must give up the temptation subtly to guide the individual, and must concentrate on one purpose only; that of providing deep understanding and acceptance of the attitudes consciously held at this moment by the client as he explores step by step into the dangerous areas which he has been denying to consciousness (Rogers, 1951, p. 30).

I do, however, have trouble with Roger's use of the word "must." Diagnosis, evaluation, and assessment don't have to be cold callous insensitive skills. These skills are actually best formulated and utilized in relationship to the reflections, experiences, and reports of the client. I don't think they need to be completely discarded and can be part of a warm, empathic interaction. This interaction should actually sharpen these traditional skills.

Further, there is the reality of insurance requirements and institutional procedures. It is more than possible to involve clients in meeting the requirements, provided they are capable. There are those who can't communicate at such formal levels.

The person-centered therapist can best be empathic by receiving the perceptions of the client. In this, they need to be received with the same integrity as the therapist receives his/her own perceptions of experiences. In doing so, it does not mean the therapist necessarily will experience what the client experiences. However, it does suggest the possibility that the therapist may have similar experiences. Being empathic acknowledges the client's feelings and experiences with the same integrity as the therapist's. This recognizes the client's experiences as being as valid and important as the therapist's. The person-centered therapist treats that world with dignity and respect.

Communicating Empathic Understanding

The empathic response is a major part of empathy. Rogers (1957) position held, "The therapist experiences an empathic understanding of the client's internal frame of reference and endeavors to communicate this experience to the client" (p. 221).

Barbara Brodley (1977) wrote, "An empathic understanding response can be a restatement, a rephrasing, a summary or a response which involves elaboration" (p. 6). According to Brodley any other response is subject to distortion by the client or the therapist.

"The empathic understanding response is fundamentally a transformation of the client's communication inside the mind and experience of the therapist. A transformation involves a change of form without altering value or meaning. In this context a transformation involves the therapist in taking the meaning of his client's expression into himself and understanding it in the terms of his own covert symbols. On the basis of the transformation the therapist may communicate outwardly, usually with language, in a way that seems likely to communicate to the client" (Brodley, p. 6).

This model has been criticized. As indicated above, reflection stirred a stereotype that concerned Rogers. I had a supervisor who shared the following illustration:

Client: I feel very horny.
Therapist: You feel horny.
Client: I think I'll masturbate.
Therapist: You think you'll masturbate.
(The patient began masturbating).

My supervisor did not say what the therapist did or said in response. He was trying to show how absurd he thought a dogmatic commitment to empathy as reflection was. However, had the therapist continued to adhere to such a radical stereotypical version of reflection, he would have masturbated also.

I'd like to offer alternatives to Barbara Brodley's (1977) assertion, but I feel limited. Words somehow seem inadequate regarding empathic responses. This is probably because there is a nonverbal intangible aspect of this experience in therapy. It is not about the words the therapist uses. Any words that are used need to be accurate. If I tell my therapist I almost stepped on a copperhead and it scared me to death. The therapist needs to understand that it was not a black snake, nor does he or she need to take note that my fear apparently didn't actually come close to killing me. There is part of that communication that is beyond the words.

It may be believed that empathy and communication are about being verbal. However, it is nonverbal as well. As if on cue, my cat walked into the room and meowed. There were no words. A meow is verbal I suppose, but to me, it is not. It is nonverbal communication. She looked at me as I looked back. I knew what she wanted. She wanted outside. Naively, I asked if she wanted out. I got up from my chair, and she began moving from my study to the kitchen. As I followed her, she went to the front door. When I opened it, she went out.

This was a little occasion, but in therapy, coming to hear the client produces similar human type experience. They occur person to person, instead of animal to person. Therefore, without a word being said, the client may communicate sadness or joy. In being empathic, the therapist without a word experiences that sadness or joy, and the client knows it.

Consequently, it is obvious that I am asserting that the process of being empathic has both verbal and nonverbal forms of communication. Empathy is a process which communicates. Communication goes hand in hand with empathy. There is no empathy without it.

Empathy and Mistakes

I have come in this theme of empathy to be open to making mistakes. It is possible for the therapist to miss what the client is saying and experiencing. It is possible to fail to understand.

I think it is a serious error to limit responses to accurate empathic responses. For I am not sure that accurate empathic responses are possible without hearing from the client what is accurate. Since I as a therapist am not a mind reader, I will make mistakes as I attempt to grasp the client's perspectives.

I am concerned that fearing that I will violate the approach and the client if I don't make accurate responses restricts my interactions. Further, I assume that what I think are accurate responses are indeed accurate. Mistakes help sharpen the focus.

I also believe mistakes let the client know when the therapist really does understand. When the therapist is off the target, the client can make the necessary corrections. At least we hope the client would. It is possible the client may not be assertive enough to correct the therapist. I would hope that is where the warmth and acceptance of this approach would be helpful. The warm accepting therapist doesn't attack the defenses of the client, and thus I suspect this makes it easier for the client to say, "No, that is not correct. This is what I mean."

When I first attempted to understand what it means to be a person-centered therapist, I found reflection helpful. It is, however, I tend to use reflection spontaneously when what the client says is obvious to me. I also use it when I can't think of anything to say, and I am simply trying to get refocused. I use reflection when I very concentrated and intensely focused. In these moments, I find myself repeating what the client says, not as a puppet, but as an expression of that concentration. At times, I find a say a word or phrase expressing the client's experience before the client does. It is indeed almost as if I am the client.

I have found that reflection can also be interruptive. In Bower (1989), it was noted that clients took time to respond to the therapist's reflection. They stopped the flow of the interaction to confirm the accuracy of the restatement. They didn't appear to object to the reflections, but the reflections did interrupt the direction the client was taking.

I tend to think that the positive potential of reflection has outweighed the negative possibilities. The verbal response does help communicate that the therapist understands and thus fulfills Rogers (1957) condition concerning empathy.

A Way Toward Being Empathic

There are several aspects of empathy as a process. First, empathy is entering the world of the client. A standard statement I have heard in demonstrations of the approach has been, "Begin any place you like." These words and the presence of the therapist begin that process of entering the world of the client. Any remark may be part of that entrance. I want to expand that to the profound nonverbal remark, silence. Silence says, I am prepared to hear you rather to have you hear me.

A theme in this is treating the client's world as my world. As I hold my world dear, so I hold the world of the client important. As I seek to understand myself, I seek to understand the client. I may fail in both. That is at times I am pretty hard on myself seeing my faults, making condescending remarks to myself. This is not acceptable in therapy. I also use self talk to motivate myself. More than once I have said, Doug, you have got to stop beating yourself up." I wonder, is this so inappropriate with the self-defeating client if the client has stated what he or she regards as self-defeating.

I see also another theme, that of entering the world of the other as if my world was the other person's world. I am not sure there is a whole lot of difference here. It is still about showing respect as I would value the client. In addition, I would seek to understand the extension of my world which is the accepting of my world by the client.

Yet, I am unsatisfied with my descriptions of these two positions. I have ah-ha experiences and attempt to write them out. However, by the time the words start being typed, the "ah-has" get away. I am left feeling awkward in my descriptions.

Empathy is about understanding the world of the client as if it was my own. It is about understanding the client as if my world is the client's world. It boggles my mind to push on the differences and the similarities.

Years ago, I was working with a client who had been separated from his wife. In my ignorance I asked, "Where is your wife living?" He stated that she was living over a hundred miles a way. This was a discovery. It spoke of a greater distance than if she had been living across town. It spoke of separation. She was not living where it was easy for him to be tempted to see here. It didn't speak of whether he made that decision, or she did. At the time I don't remember wanting to or actually asking who initiated this distance. However, the answer would have said something else about the client's world and his perceptions of it. With further questions, the client demonstrated his own reluctance and fear to travel so far to see his wife only to be attacked verbally and physically by his wife's relatives. This said more. It spoke of his fears, and it said that his separated wife had moved into the protection of her relatives.

The primary means of understanding is though is listening. As I started grappling with understanding the person-centered approach, I moved towards giving up my belief that a good therapist needs to confront the client, honing in the client's experience in such as way as to trigger catharsis. Jerold Bozarth who was my supervisor at the time made an important suggestion among many others. It would prove to be one of the most influential suggestions given to me in any supervision: "Listen," he said.

I have come to be more interested in the perceptions of the client as they develop in our relationship. I would rather not even have a history from a former therapist. I don't want to be biased by it. I want to find out for myself what the client has to say. In addition, I have come to believe that new sets of presuppositions from the client emerge in the context of the therapeutic relationship. These are uncluttered by my assumptions, especially if I am not polluting them with my assumptions. Furthermore, they are especially uncluttered, if I am focused what the client is presenting. These perceptions and how I am impacted by them inform me about the world of the client.

Summary

This was a presentation of the process of empathy. It rested in part on my grasp of Rogers' early articulations of empathy. Rogers and other restated numerous times through the years.

Empathy is receiving, in so far as is possible, "the internal frame reference of the client, to perceive the world as the client sees it, to perceive the client himself as he is seen by himself, to lay aside all perceptions from the external frame of reference while doing so, and to communicate something of the empathic understanding to the client," the person-centered therapist understanding to the client" (Rogers, 1951, p. 29). Empathy is a sentient aspect of the approach.

References

Bower, D. W. (1989). *The attributes of five person-centered therapists.* Unpublished doctoral dissertation, University of Georgia, Athens, Georgia.

Bozarth, J. D. (1984). Beyond reflection: Emergent modes of empathy. In R. E. Levant, & J. M. Shlien (Eds.), *Client-centered therapy and the person-centered approach* (pp. 59-75). New York: Praeger.

Bozarth, J. D. (1996). A silent young man: The case of Jim Brown. In B. A. Farber, D. C. Brink, & P. M. Raskin (Eds.). *The psychotherapy of Carl Rogers: Cases and commentary* (pp. 240-250). New York: The Guilford Press.

Bozarth, J. D. (1998). *Person-centered therapy: A revolutionary paradigm.* Ross-on-Wye: PCCS Books.

Bozarth, J. D., & Brodley, B. T. (1991). Actualization: A functional concept in client-centered therapy. *Journal of Social and Behavior Change*, 6(5), 45-49.

Brodley, B. T. (1977). *The empathic understanding response process* (unpublished manuscript).

Rogers, C. R. (1951). *Client-centered therapy.* Boston: Houghton Mifflin Co.

Rogers, C. R. (1957). The necessary and sufficient conditions of therapeutic personality change. Reprinted in H. Kirschenbaum, V. L. Henderson (Eds.) (1989). *The Carl Rogers reader.* Boston: Houghton Mifflin Co., pp. 219-235.

Rogers, C. R. (1961). *On becoming a person.* Boston: Houghton Mifflin Co.

Rogers, C. R. (1977). *On personal power.* New York, New York: Delta Books.

Rogers, C. R. (1980). *A way of being.* Boston: Houghton Mifflin Co.

Rogers, C. R. (1986). Reflection of feelings and transference. Reprinted in H. Kirschenbaum, V. L. Henderson (Eds.) (1989).

The Carl Rogers reader. Boston: Houghton Mifflin Co., pp. 219-235.

Shlien, J. M. (1970). Phenomenology and personality. In J. T. Hart, & T. M. Tomlinson (Eds.), *New directions in client-centered therapy* (pp. 95-128). Boston: Houghton Mifflin Company.

Congruence/Genuineness:

The Core Condition

When I started investigating my interests in the person-centered approach in the 80's, I was concerned that the person-centered therapist might become minimized as a person. The therapist might lose him or herself during therapy. Actually, my dissertation (Bower, 1989) contained reports that the therapist "disappeared." I was afraid that the therapist's own feelings, thoughts and experiences would be overlooked.

In my opinion, the condition of congruence/genuineness is about the therapist as a person and of course about the client as a person. This person cannot, should not get lost during therapy.

Rogers stated that one of the conditions of therapy (1957) included a client who came "in a state of incongruence." The client thus is out of sync with his or her self. The therapist was seen in that article as being in a state of "congruence."

A Definition of Congruence

Congruence has been defined (Merriam-Webster's) as "the quality or state of agreeing or coinciding." The related word, congruous, is defined as "being in agreement, harmony, or correspondence." "To come together," is the idea.

I have come to define congruence as the state of being in touch with the self one truly is.

Rogers described congruence as follows:

"The more the therapist is herself in the relationship, putting up no professional front or personal facade, the greater is the likelihood that the client will change and grow in a constructive manner. It means that the therapist is openly being the feelings and attitudes that are flowing within at the moment. The term transparent catches the flavor of this element - the therapist makes herself transparent to the client; the client can see right through what the therapist is in the relationship; the client experiences no holding back on the part of the therapist. As for the therapist, what she is experiencing is available to awareness, can be lived in the relationship, and be communicated if appropriate. Thus there is a close matching, or congruence, among what is being experienced at the gut level, what is present in awareness, and what is expressed to the client" (Rogers, 1977, p. 9).

The State of Being Congruent

I consider two terms that are essential to Rogersl view of congruence are "self" and "self concept." There are other concepts such as "self ideal." However, I regard it as being closely related to "self-concept."

Self

I risk some redundancy here from the section of self-actualization.

Self can be described as an individual's self-experience which is "any event or entity in the phenomenal field discriminated by the individual which is also discriminated as 'self,' 'me,' 'I,' or related thereto" (Rogers, 1959, p. 200). The self is the actual experience of the person, including thoughts and emotions. The self is comprised of the total experiences of the person.

Somatic experiences are an important part of this total. All somatic functions contribute to the formulation and maintenance of the self and if one's physiology is altered, the self is altered.

Another aspect important to the self is the social environment. The social environment is influential on the self which is impossible without an environment. The people a person encounters play a part in the formulation of the self. The social does not formulate the self; the self is actualized only by its self. However, as the social environmental changes, the self is impacted by these changes. Thus, the loss of a loved one or a major move can and will play a part in changing the self as the self adjusts to a new set of events and experiences.

The mental or psychological is another component of the self. This aspect includes the physiology of the brain, without which there would be no mental or psychological functioning. There would be no discrimination process regarding the events or entities in the person's phenomenal field. Not would there be any thought processes or emotional processes.

Self-Concept

The self-concept is "the organized, consistent conceptual gestalt composed of perceptions of the characteristics of the 'I' or 'me' and the perceptions of the relationships of the 'I' or 'me' to others and to various aspects of life, together with the values attached to these perceptions" (Rogers, 1959, p. 200). The self-concept is that which the person perceives him or herself to be. This perception is influenced by others' perceptions of the person, sometimes to the extent that the person strives to become the person of those perceptions. In this case he or she denies his or her own self. In any case, the self-concept is the self as perceived.

The self and the self-concept match-up in the state of congruence. If I had worked with the self ideal, I would also assert that this self ideal would be in sync with whom the person truly is. The person would accept him or herself as is, not trying to be a person that he or she is not.

Incongruence a Key to Understanding Congruence

Incongruence is the state of being out of touch with the self that one truly is. For instance, I fancied myself to be a fast runner. I wasn't. I also didn't see myself as physically attractive. I wasn't Mr. All-American looking, but my football picture in the high school year book looks pretty good.

It is my experience or my observation that people who have come to me for counseling have lost touch with how to make themselves feel the way they want to feel, or believe the things that they want to believe. They simply are out of touch with how to feel good about themselves.

A key to understanding congruence is Rogers' definition of incongruence. "Incongruence is a discrepancy . . . between the self as perceived, and the actual experience of the organism. Thus the individual may perceive himself as having characteristics a, b, and c, and experiencing feelings x, y, and z. An accurate symbolization of his experience would, however, indicate characteristics c, d, and e, and feelings v, w, x" (Rogers, 1959, p. 203).

When a person is incongruent, there is a difference between the experiences which comprise the actual self and the perceptions of those self experiences. The experiences are blocked from awareness. Rogers says that this state creates problems "of tension and internal confusion . . ." (p. 203).

<u>The Congruent Therapist</u>

When the therapist is congruent there is no discrepancy between the self and the self-concept, at least during the time of therapeutic interaction. The two, self and self-concept, are in relative harmony or agreement.

Rogers did not view being congruent as being a constant state for any therapist or any person. He argued that inasmuch as the therapist is congruent in the therapeutic situation, growth can take place within the client. The self-actualization process, the process of perceiving the self in relationship to its real experiences, can be maximized in relationship with a congruent therapist.

"It is only by providing the genuine reality which is in me, that the other person can successfully seek for the reality in him. I have found this to be true even when the attitudes I feel are not attitudes with which I am pleased, or attitudes which seem conducive to a good relationship. It seems extremely important to be real" (Rogers, 1961, p. 33).

In my opinion this is the weakest link in the theory. Not on account of Rogers' statement, but by reason of concepts such as unconditional positive regard and nonjudgmentalness. It has often seemed to me that my colleagues in the approach dread real experiences. There doesn't seem to a willingness to accept the genuine judgmental or negative regard of the therapist. The number of times I have heard, "you aren't being person-centered is left uncounted. You are being "judgmental" defies counting.

I don't espouse beating up clients, but I know I have seen clients I didn't like or have warm feelings about. This always seems important to note. However, this note is not used as a club to beat myself up for failing to live up to the standards of the approach. I figure that my negative experiences may say something important about the client.

Bozarth (1998) pointed out that in the early years, congruence as genuineness was related to genuine warmth. This also seems to be related to being genuinely empathic. Personally, I haven't seen that has changed if at all, though Bozarth does seem to say that Rogers placed more emphasis on "the therapist's feelings, awareness of feelings and expression of feelings as the substance of genuineness" (p. 72). I concur, as long as those experiences aren't used against the client, or against the therapist. "Negative thoughts, feelings and attitudes need particularly to be acknowledged by the therapist" (Thorne, 1992, p. 37). Early in the paragraph he wrote, "Achieving this condition is not an easy task for it requires of the therapist a continuing openness to inner experience even if what is experienced poses a threat to the therapist's self-concept" (p. 37). An example of which, good nonjudgmental therapists who have unconditional positive regard don't have negative experiences towards the client.

Also, I assert that the therapist needs to be willing to struggle with wondering if any given experience on the part of the therapist is related to the therapist's own world view or says something about the client's experiences. To assume my negative regard is just my stuff, may be a mistake. Of course, to assume that it is related to the client is a mistake as well. I am simply suggesting that the therapist be open to the possibility that the therapist's experiences in relationship to the client are informative about the client's experiences.

I feel comfortable with Rogers' position that genuineness/congruence means "that the therapist is openly being the feelings and attitudes that are flowing within at the moment" (Rogers, 1980, p. 115).

The Congruent Relationship

A second aspect of congruence is evidenced in the coming together of the therapist and the client. Until the therapist is congruent with him or herself, he or she cannot be empathic with another. Since empathy is the process of entering the world of the client, it is a coming together of a client and a therapist. In essence, empathy is the therapist's becoming congruent, as much as possible, with the client. In the person-centered approach, the therapist who is congruent can then be congruent with another, the client. The therapist can thus let the client be him or herself whether the therapist actually likes the client or not (But that is another issue).

The Therapist as Real and Genuine

The congruent therapist accepts his/her own thoughts, feelings, and experiences. He/she is real. He/she is genuine. He/she experiences anger, sexual urges, depression, joy, love, and hate. Being aware of these experiences, the congruent therapist can accept these as being a significant part of his or her self. It is the denial of one's experiences which is the basis for incongruence.

The therapist who can accept him or herself and his or her experiences can accept these same kinds of experiences as being a part of others. This acceptance makes it possible to be congruent with the client. The therapist, who can empathize, being secure enough with his or her own world, is not overwhelmed by the feelings, thoughts and experiences of the client's world. He or she can thus become empathically one with the client.

The client can perceive the congruent therapist as being genuine and real. The client experiences the therapist for what he is. For in the therapist being open to personal experiences and open to the world of the client, the client is touched by those. "Each of us knows individuals whom we somehow trust because we sense they are being what they are, that we are dealing with the person himself, not with a polite or professional front. It is this quality of congruence that we sense which research has found to be associated with successful therapy" (Rogers, 1961, p. 61).

Rogers makes this genuineness sound almost mystical when referring to "individuals whom we somehow trust" because we somehow we mysteriously sense this genuineness. I do not believe that it is a matter of mystery. Genuineness can be communicated both verbally and nonverbally. "The feelings the therapist is experiencing are available to him, available to his awareness, and he is able to live these feelings, be them, and able to communicate them if appropriate" (p. 61).

A Missing Dimension

Tapes by person-centered therapists (Bower, 1989) revealed that the therapists tended not share their own experiences with their clients. Often disclosure seems to go no further than an occasional admission that the therapist is having difficulty comprehending what client has said. The tendency seems intended to reflect the client's perception without sharing the inner impact that the client has had on the therapist.

However, Rogers is willing to share himself with his clients. In the "Gloria" film (Rogers, 1965), he said, "I think you'd make a pretty nice daughter." In a film illustrating his group theory, he wiped tears from his eyes when interacting with a young woman. In writing about confrontation, Rogers demonstrates this further:

"I tend to confront individuals on specifics of their behavior. 'I don't like the way you chatter on. Seems to me you give each message three of four times. I wish you would stop when you've completed your message.' 'To me you seem sort of like silly putty. Someone seems to reach you, to make a dent in you, but then it all springs back into place as though you hadn't been touched.'

And I like to confront another person only with feelings I am willing to claim as my own. These may at times be very strong. 'Never in my life have I been so pissed off at a group as I am at this one.' Or, to one man in the group, 'I woke up this morning feeling, 'I never want to see you again.'

To attack a person's defenses seems to me judgmental. If one says, 'You're hiding a lot of hostility,' or 'You are being highly intellectual probably because you are afraid of your own feelings,' I believe such judgments and diagnoses are the opposite of facilitative. If, however, what I perceive as the person's coldness frustrates me or his intellectualizing irritates me, or his brutality to another person angers me, then I would like to face him with the frustration or the irritation or the anger that exists in me. To me this is very important" (Rogers, 1970, p. 58-59).

This approach is very open, genuine and real. I know what is happening with the therapist. The real and genuine therapist can and will have feelings during therapy, as the client's world makes an impact on the therapist's world. There will be feelings present, and not always pleasant ones. There can be experiences of fatigue or feelings of impatience. However, it does not seem to be a pattern for person-centered therapists to verbally claim these experiences during therapy, despite the theoretical and practical example of Rogers himself.

I disagree though with Rogers's assertion that his way of presenting his thoughts and experiences are less likely to attack defenses. It has been my experience to see people in a variety of settings, not just therapy, become defensive when people speak to them the way Rogers presented himself above.

The experiences of the therapist can be the basis of valuable empathic responses. Bozarth (1992) argued for attending to one's self during therapy as well as attending to the client. The reason for this is that what the therapist experiences during therapy can be related to the experiences of the client. One of my clients began sessions with "I don't have anything to talk about." I tended to feel uncomfortable during the beginning of the sessions. "What are we going to do this hour?" I wondered. I would think that my thoughts and feelings of boredom could have been utilized in an empathic encounter, but unfortunately, I did not check my experiences out with the client. Thus, I remain to this day unable to confirm my suspicion. However, in another client, I encountered a very hostile and agitated person. I experienced feelings of anger, hostility and agitation. I also experienced fear. I now believe that my experiences were related to the experiences of the client.

Implications

I believe that the states of genuineness and transparency can open doors to communication therapy. I cannot, however, believe that it is possible always to be empathic and maintain unconditional positive regard of a client. Since, I no longer believe in unconditional positive regard, it seems to be a facade to take the role of the stereotypical person-centered therapist. To be real might mean saying to the client, "I don't understand what you are saying." Or, "I am feeling very angry right now." Or, "I am beginning to feel like I am being manipulated." I do not believe that these examples violate the principle or intention of Rogers' theory. They may very well be appropriate genuine responses.

I believe the excessive use of reflection can handicap the communication of the therapist.

Bozarth (1984) expressed a variety of concerns about the issue of reflection. For me, the client does not know what the therapist feels, thinks or experiences. In reflection, the client encounters only the reflection of him or herself and not his or her impact on another person. For instance, a person's behavior might stimulate irritation in others. With the exclusive use of reflection, the client might never know that his or her behavior is met with irritation by others or the therapist.

I believe that the concept of congruence holds tremendous potential for dealing with major problems with clients. "I like you and I don't want to see you go to jail for murder," is a real and genuine response. "I'd miss you and it would hurt to know that you killed yourself," is also genuine and real.

I believe that a great deal of criticism of the person-centered approach can be averted by allowing the therapist to be him or herself, instead of insisting that he or she become exclusively reflective and thus limited to a stereotypical approximation of empathy. Again, this is not about giving permission to therapists to genuinely violate humanitarian principles or ethical guidelines.

Summary

Rogers' notion of congruence has two aspects: a coming together of the therapist's self and the self-concept, and the subsequent ability for the therapist to enter into the world of the client, genuinely accept the client and be viewed as being real by the client.

The therapist has a wealth of experiences during therapy. These experiences may be related to the experiences of the client, and thus, they can be utilized to help the therapist understand the inner world of the client.

What has impressed me about the person-centered theory are the potentially many different ways of being congruent and genuine. These possible expressions need to be explored, to expand the repertoire of presently reflective and empathic responses available to the therapist.

References

Bower, D. W. (1989). *The attributes of five person-centered therapists.* Unpublished doctoral dissertation, University of Georgia, Athens, Georgia.

Bozarth, J. D. (1984). Beyond reflection: Emergent modes of empathy. In, R. F. Levant, & J. M Shlien (Eds.). *Client-centered therapy and the person-centered approach: New directions in theory, research, and practice.* New York: Praeger.

Bozarth, J. D. (1992). Coterminous intermingling of doing and being in person-centered therapy. *The Person-Centered Journal,* 1 (1), 12-20.

Merriam-Webster's Collegiate Dictionary. (1994) Electronic Edition, v. 1.5: Merriam-Webster, Inc.

Rogers, C. R. (1959) A theory of therapy, personality, and interpersonal relationships, as developed in the client-centered framework." In S. Koch (Ed.) *Psychology: A study of a science, Vol. III: Formulations of the person and the social context.* New York: McGraw-Hill.

Rogers, C. R. (1961). *On becoming a person.* Boston: Houghton Mifflin.

Rogers, C. R. (1965). *Three approaches to psychotherapy 1.* Psychological Films. [Film].

Rogers, C. R. (1970). *On encounter groups.* New York: Perennial Library.

Rogers, C. R. (1977). *On personal power.* New York: Delta..

Rogers, C. R. (1980). *A way of being.* Boston: Houghton Mifflin Co.

Thorne, B. (1992). *Carl Rogers.* London: Sage Publications.

Psycho-Social Assessment and the PCA

In 1986 or 87, I went before a committee of people who were to evaluate my performance regarding my competence to receive a graduate degree in Pastoral Counseling. I had been studying part-time for nearly 7 years and was ready to leave.

I presented my client from a person-centered approach perspective. I had been studying with Jerold Bozarth and had come to deeply appreciate the person-centered approach to therapy.

I presented my tape of a session, a write-up that I felt reflected my grasp of the client in relationship to the person-centered approach, and even offered a Barrett-Leonard Relationship Inventory as done by myself and the client. I felt I was consistent with the approach. The client felt I was consistent with the approach. At least, the client was satisfied with her counseling. And my score on the Barrett-Leonard Relationship Inventory was at least as high as those who were adherents of the approach.

To my chagrin, I failed the evaluation. I hadn't prepared an extensive psycho-social assessment of the client. My presentation was not consistent with the psycho-dynamic model that I had been trained in. And I hadn't presented a client that I had seen at least 19 times. I may be over on the number of times, and even if I am accurate on it, I wouldn't have a clue why the number 20 was sacred.

We had an ensuing fight that resulted in a stalemate and I lost the degree. I felt that it was important to stick-up for my newly founded person-centered orientation. And I felt it was unethical for me as a practitioner to attempt to use a model of counseling and psychotherapy that I didn't believe in.

The battle lost, I have refused to have anything to do with the school that denied me a degree based on one exam that wasn't even mentioned as a requirement for a degree.

That being said, I have an appreciation for psycho-social assessments. However, I personally still do not use them. The reason for this is that I believe healing does not come from psycho-social assessments. It comes in relationship to the core conditions of empathy, acceptance, and genuineness. A good psycho-social assessment takes weeks. Why waste that time gathering information for a formal document? Instead, why not offer that which has the most potential for helping a client right now?

Rogers (1986) wrote of a significant contrast between the more directive models which emphasize psycho-social assessments:

"Seeing the human organism as essentially positive in nature – is profoundly radical. It flies in the face of traditional psychoanalysis, runs counter to the Christian tradition, and is opposed to the philosophy of most institutions, including our educational institutions. In the psychoanalytic theory our core is seen as untamed, wild, destructive. In Christian theology we are 'conceived in sin,' and evil by nature. In our institutions that individual is seen as untrustworthy. Persons must be guided, corrected, disciplined, punished, so that they will not follow the pathway set by their nature" (p. 127).

In itself this quote is more about the faith in human potential than about psycho-social assessment. However, the psycho-social assessment is about getting past the superficial facades and defenses of the client in order to accurate capture what is really going on with the client.

Rogers was not a supporter of this kind of formality in dealing with clients. In fact, I detect a bit of hostility towards this model. It would appear to me that he connects the psycho-social assessment to the politics of the professional. "It has to do with the maneuvers, the strategies and tactics, witting or unwitting, by which such power and control over one's own life and other's lives is sought and gained – or shared or relinquished" (Rogers, 1977, p. 4).

The client has to participate in the psycho-social process because the professional helper demands it. It is expected. Good clients, participate willingly. Defensive clients don't and thus are not good clients.

Based on my experience, I have seen the coercion surrounding the use of psycho-social assessments and diagnostic procedures. So I find myself in agreement with Rogers' concerns.

However, I see another side. That is, just because there are power-mongers in the fields of psychology, psychiatry, and psychotherapy, doesn't mean that there is a warm intention regarding the use of formal assessment.

A good example comes from Sullivan (1954). "Since the field of psychiatry has been defined as the study of interpersonal relations, and since it has been alleged that this is a perfectly valid area for the application of scientific method, we have come to the conclusion that the data of psychiatry arise only in participant observation (p. 3). Thus, a good psycho-social evaluation arises in relationship to studying a particular kind of interpersonal relationship, counseling, psychotherapy, or psychological or psychiatric evaluation.

Groth-Marnat (2003) stated, "Psychological assessment attempts to evaluate an individual in a problem situation so that the information derived from the can somehow help with the problem" (p. 3). Surely, the intentions are good and certainly beyond reproach ethically. They contrast though with the "nondirective" model. In this model, individuals have vast resources for personal growth and don't need direct intervention. Rogers (1977), sees assessment protocols as externally imposed from a professional. It is clear that Groth-Marnat sees it an important part of helping people in trouble.

Ey & Hersen (2004) seem to affectionately look at psychological assessment from being the investigation of a detective. Referring to popular television detectives like Columbo, they suggest that discovering problems of a client tantamount to seeking clues to the problems a client might experience. They do offer a rather positive slant to this saying, "the ability to carry out a thorough investigation of a client's presenting problem is key to psychotherapy . . . Clinicians use assessment to understand what brings the client to therapy, what types of treatment might be appropriate, and monitor whether interventions are helpful" (p. 3).

I can appreciate that. However, I find that asking the client about these things rather than Weschler or the MMPI is very revealing. Moreover, I would disagree that a psychological assessment tells what "treatment" might be appropriate. That comes from knowing treatment modalities and how they match up with particular clients and disorders. I would concern that in this model of assessment discovering what is wrong would thus lead to treatment selection. However, I see treatment as a different part of psychotherapy.

I still appreciate the friendliness of many professionals for psychological assessment, but I am not convinced that it is essential to good psychotherapy. Thus, the above positions and similar ones don't change my mind about my own use of a formal psycho-social assessment. It does say that it doesn't have to be the cold calculating power stuff associated with a professional taking on the role of an expert. The expert role has long been viewed dimly in the person-centered approach (Bozarth, 1998).

Personally, in my own initial explorations with psycho-social assessment, I didn't find that formal protocols and tests led me to discover anything about the client I wouldn't find by having an open empathic relationship with a client. They may have offered a more formal way of speaking to the client's problems using professional jargon, but I didn't find psycho-social assessment informative.

Several Models Emphasize Pathology

Groth-Marnat (2003) pointed to number of evaluation instruments that are designed to find out what is wrong with a person. These include the Wechsler Intelligence Scales, Wechsler Memory Scales, the Minnesota Multiphasic Personality Inventory, Millon Clinical Multiaxial Inventory, California Psychological Inventory, Rorschach, and the Thematic Apperception Test. There are others of course.

My experience of these instruments is that no one has mental health. Everyone has mental illness.

In addition, all these instruments of evaluation require special training. They are so complex that there is a fear that they will be misused in the hands of the undertrained.

In the person-centered approach, the client is the expert concerning the problem or problems. The therapist is the learner, but learns from the client rather than professional assessment protocols and instruments.

The Models Are Still Based on Presuppositions from the 20th Century

Freud and psychoanalysis still lurk over the psychotherapeutic community. The insistence for psycho-social assessment has to come from that model of therapy. It has indeed been greatly modified by the rise of behaviorism, cognitive-behaviorism, and humanism. Managed Care and the insurance model has altered it further. The basis for assessment has its roots in the beginnings of psychotherapy, at least from the time of the Freudians.

I am not prepared to articulate how Freud lingers. Nor am I prepared to speak to how later 20th century models influenced the evolution of psycho-social assessment. Just an effort to speak to these is bigger than one chapter in a book. They probably also require more involvement in their development than I am willing to give.

The only model of psychotherapy that moves away from 20th century presuppositions about psycho-social assessment is the person-centered approach Rogers (1977). It is not necessary for therapy. In itself, psycho-social assessment is directly not therapeutic.

Gathering information on the client in the person-centered approach is based on what one learns from the client. It is not based on standardized practices, protocols, methodologies, or testing instruments. What can I learn from the client? How does the client speak of his or her problems?

The Presence Always Clouds the Past

I am satisfied that Rogers and others didn't emphasize this argument for rejecting psycho-social assessment. Rather, the rejection is apparently more based on rejecting the role of the therapist as expert (Rogers, 1942; Rogers, 1980; Bozarth, 1992). The notion that assessment is unnecessary also plays a role in rejecting it (Rogers, 1942: Rogers, 1961; AllPsych, 2003). (Rogers, 1942) also indicated that there was more emphasis upon the "immediate situation" rather than the "individual's past."

I assert that the present clouds that past. This may be more of a Whitehead framework than a humanistic one. The present is always made possible because of the prehension of the past. However, due to the new twist the present puts on the moment, it is different from the past. When reflecting on the past, clients will always interpret the past through present perspectives, and the past will always be colored by those perspectives.

Since I hold this to be true, even if the client reflects on the past, I always understand that reflection as saying a great deal about the client's experience in the present moment. So I take notice of anger, sadness, joy, celebration, or other experiences the client shares in relationship to reflecting on the past.

The Therapist Will Find Out Important Information

A good therapist will always eventually find out the most significant aspects of the client through therapy anyway. I am ambivalent about using the word "good" in the above phrase. Bad therapists can find out important information as well. Besides, who defines "good"? What is a good therapist? The presupposition is that a good therapist is one who maintains the core conditions of empathy, acceptance, and genuineness.

The genuine therapist who receives (accepts) the perspectives of the client by entering into the world of the client (empathy), will learn about what is important to the client.

This does not mean that the client will share every thing with the therapist. It does not mean that client is responsible for sharing everything with the therapist. The client is free to withhold anything. The client is free to share anything.

This is a variation of the Rogers (1980) notion that "the individual in this nurturing climate is free to choose any direction, but actually selects positive and constructive ways." Free to withhold important information, experiences, thoughts, and ideas, clients tend to share important information, etc.

Rather than share that information in the formal protocol established externally by a therapist who in all likelihood adopted it from an external source, the client share information based on how he or she sees its importance.

This minimizes defensiveness as the client doesn't have to guard against premature intrusions from the therapist. There isn't pressure to open up to the therapist. Thus, the client is more open to share with the therapist.

No Evidence That Psycho-social Assessment Heals

There is no evidence that psycho-social assessment heals, treats, or is therapeutic in terms of demonstrating care to the client.

It may be argued that a good psycho-social assessment leads to determining treatment. This is not specifically stated in some traditional frameworks of psychotherapy like (Kolb, 1968; English & Finch, 1964), but strongly implied. Personally, though, I found Kolb's material on the psychiatrist- patient relationship rather warm and open seeking to communicate understanding and minimizing defensiveness with the client. This seems congruent with Harry Stack Sullivan's (1954) position on the psychiatrist as participant observer. It also advocated for a nonjudgmental engagement with the client. (English & Finch) also communicate this warm approach to dealing with the total person called the patient. There is a rejection of the authoritarian attitude towards patients. None of these classical resources mentioned above overtly advocate that history taking is about preparing for offering treatment. However, clearly all the above resources are associated with preparing and understanding of what ails the client so that the psychotherapist (in these classical resources the psychiatrist) can offer treatment to the client.

However, they all assert that in certain conditions such as psychotic episodes a history is impossible to obtain. Thus, personally, I see the history as unnecessary to the therapy. I thus fall back on the notion that a therapist seeking to enter the world of the client will learn the stuff of psycho-social or traditional history. It doesn't have to be a formalized process.

Hone In On What Is Directly Therapeutic

Thus, providing that which is therapeutic is the essential aspect of therapy. Instead of wasting time using cold aloof instruments of assessment, go ahead and offer therapy adjusting it as needed to new discoveries during the therapeutic process with the client. It is real clear from Rogers (1942, 1961, & 1980) and all his works, and those of colleagues that find the approach therapeutic that certain conditions facilitate change, or are what I called in another section soothing.

A Reality: Psycho-Social Assessments Are Required in Institutional Scenarios

Given the reluctance of the approach to play the role of expert, what can be done? Given the preference to allow the client to be self-directive, what can we do?

The answer is simply stated. Involve the clients in working with the protocols. What are their answers to the questions? What is their diagnosis? The therapist may need to share the various criteria for diagnosis. There is nothing secretive about the criterion. It is easily obtained in any bookstore or on the Internet. Clients can even fill out the forms if they are able. There may be clients who have physical limitations who cannot fill out the necessary forms for insurance or institutional purposes. The therapist can do that.

The final position though is that unless psycho-social assessment is mandated by an institution, there really is no need for it. The basic premise here is to offer that which is therapeutic from the start of the therapy rather than spend energy with unnecessary protocols.

References

Allpsych. (2003). *Psychology biographies: Carl Rogers.* Allpsych online: Virtual psychology classroom: AllPsych and Heffner Media Group, Inc. http://allpsych.com/biographies/rogers.html

Bozarth, J. D. (1992). Coterminous intermingling of doing and being in person-centered therapy. *The Person-Centered Journal,* 1(1), 12-20.

Bozarth, J. D. (1998). *Person-centered therapy: A revolutionary paradigm.* Ross-on-Wye: PCCS Books.

English O. S., & Finch, S. M. (1964). *Introduction to psychiatry.* New York: W. W. Norton & Company.

Groth-Marnat, G. (2003). *Handbook of psychological assessment.* Hoboken, New Jersey: John Wiley & Sons.

Kolb, L. C. (1968). *Noyes' modern clinical psychiatry.* Philadelphia: W. B. Sanders Company.

Rogers, C. R. (1942). *Counseling and psychotherapy.* Boston: Houghton Mifflin.

Rogers, C. R. (1961). *On becoming a person.* Boston: Houghton Mifflin.

Rogers, C. R. (1977). *On personal power.* New York: A Delta Book.

Sullivan, H. S. (1954). *The psychiatric interview.* H. S. Perry & M. L. Gawel (Eds.). New York: W. W. Norton & Company.

The Person-Centered Approach as Ethics

John Wesley (1703-1791) offered the following "Rules of Conduct" for Christians:

Do all the good you can,
By all the means you can,
In all the ways you can,
In all the places you can,
At all the times you can,
To all the people you can,
As long as ever you can.

Dictionary.com (Ethics, n.d.) defined ethics as "1. (used with a singular or plural verb) a system of moral principles: the ethics of a culture. 2. the rules of conduct recognized in respect to a particular class of human actions or a particular group, culture, etc.: medical ethics; Christian ethics. 3. moral principles, as of an individual: His ethics forbade betrayal of a confidence. 4. (usually used with a singular verb) that branch of philosophy dealing with values relating to human conduct, with respect to the rightness and wrongness of certain actions and to the goodness and badness of the motives and ends of such actions." Gleaning from this to psychotherapy in general, and the person-centered approach to therapy and helping in particular, I think it is safe to assert that person-centered ethics is a system of principles, conduct, which pertain to relating to others.

Institutional Approach to Ethics

In this framework, an organization such as a state government or a professional organization stands behind ethical expectations.

I will present first what I will call categories of the ethical standards of the American Psychological Association as they are presented in an annual report (Report, 2006). I won't attempt to explain any these categories.

Cases adjudicated in other jurisdictions
    Felony conviction
    Loss of licensure
    Expulsion from state association
    Malpractice
    Other Dual relationship
    Sexual misconduct, adult
    Sexual misconduct, minor
    Sexual harassment
    Nonsexual dual relationship Inappropriate professional practice
    Child custody
    Hospitalization
    Hypnosis
    Outside competence
    Controlling client
    Inappropriate response to crisis
    Confidentiality
    Inappropriate follow-up/termination
    Test misuse
    Insurance/fee problems
    Inappropriate professional relations
    Other
Inappropriate research, teaching, or administrative practice
    Authorship controversies/credits
    Improper research techniques
    Plagiarism
    Biasing data
    Grading/violation of student rights

Termination/supervision
Absence of timely evaluations
Discrimination
Animal research subjects' welfare
Other Inappropriate public statements
Misuse of media
False, fraudulent, or misleading
Did not correct misrepresentation
Public allegation about colleague
Other
Failure to uphold standards of the profession
Response to APA Ethics Committee
Adherence to standards
Other Total cases

Second, I will present basic concepts from the Institutional position of government. In this case, the Georgia Code (Title 43, 2007): "43-10A-5 (d) The board shall adopt a code of ethics to govern the behavior of persons licensed under this chapter"

This code of ethics presented in the Rules of Georgia Composite Board of Professional Counselors, Social Workers and Marriage and Family Therapists includes the following basic principles:"

* Responsibility to Clients (135-7-.01)
(1) A licensee's primary professional responsibility is to the client.

* Integrity (135-7-.02)
(1) The licensee shall act in accordance with the highest standards of professional integrity and competence.

* Confidentiality (135-7-.03)
(1) The licensee holds in confidence all information obtained at any time during the course of a professional relationship, beginning with the first professional contact.

* Responsibility to Colleagues (135-7-.04)

(1) The licensee respects the rights and responsibilities of professional colleagues and, as the employee of an organization, remains accountable as an individual to the ethical principles of the profession.

* Assessment Instruments (135-7-.05)

(1) When using assessment instruments or techniques, the licensee shall make every effort to promote the welfare and best interests of the client.

* Research (135-7-.06)

(1) The licensee recognizes that research activities must be conducted with full respect for the rights and dignity of participants and with full concern for their welfare.

* Advertising and Professional Representation (135-7-.07)

(1) The licensee adheres to professional rather than commercial standards when making known their availability for professional services, expertise, and techniques available.

NonInstitutional

From this standpoint, a person, not an organization, asserts ethical expectations. These expectations are informed by professional training, societal expectations, and other persons. It is possible that these personal ethical expectations could be completely congruent with various institutional expectations. However, in the person-centered approach the ethics is based on the principles of the client and of the therapist.

Rather than having an institution formulating a code of ethics that members are expected to adhere to, the person-centered approach recognizes that persons are capable of defining and sustaining ethical principles (Rogers, 1961).

Also, rather than having an institution enforcing a code of ethics and investigating and prosecuting violations of such a code, the person-centered approach says that any given individual has the authority to speak for him or her self on matters of feeling violating.

This may appear to create some chaos in not having clearly defined rules of conduct. However, what it does is put individuals in charge of making such determinations. The consequences of violating expectations of the approach are not institutional excommunication, but there may be personal excommunication or chastisement from a community.

This though is problematic in light of the principle of unconditional positive regard which lays no conditions on being accepted. However, in fact, personal excommunication occurs. That excommunication may take the form of a person deciding not to associate with the person-centered community in light of reactions to behaviors. For instance, there was an incidence of a woman reporting to a person-centered community that someone in the person-centered community attempted to rape her. While she had legal recourse, she chose to deal with it in the community. The community struggled with the incident for some time. The final outcome was not a banishment of the person committing the atrocity, but rather that person stopped associating with person-centered communities. It was very traumatic for the victim, the perpetrator, and the community.

At this writing, the person violating the woman has not returned to the community. He was effectively excommunicated from the community by peer pressure and certainly by the complaint of the victim to the community.

It might be stated that the person is still loose in society. That is a good point. However, the person who was violated made that call. She could have taken a legal avenue and did not. In part because she was painfully aware that, in taking legal recourse all too many women are treated poorly, as if they are liars. She didn't want to be treated like that and have her testimony be a matter of public record. Nor did she want the person who violated her to be branded as a criminal by a cold insensitive system. She simply wanted justice. She reported obtaining that justice, though she still had to painfully struggle with what happened to her.

The point being is that a community of persons dealt with the situation rather than a formal system of rules, regulations, and laws.

Respect of Persons

Rogers' position on clients as persons was summarized nicely (1957a). "In my experience I have discovered man to have characteristics which seem inherent to his species, and the terms which have at different times seemed to me descriptive of these characteristics are such terms as *positive, forward-moving, constructive, realistic, trustworthy*" (p. 403).

In my own interactions with colleagues and listening to professionals in other disciplines, I have noted a pessimism regarding clients/patients, or students. The range of that pessimism included views of the other person being stupid, unteachable, difficult, stubborn, or vicious and mean-spirited. In listening to these people, I think they can make a case of a sort of innate destructive tendency in human beings. Yet, I can't say that these people reported progress with those they held such a dim view of. "Many other aspects of our culture take the view that the nature of the individual is such that he cannot be trusted – that he must be guided, instructed, rewarded, punished, and controlled by those who are wiser or higher in status" (Rogers, 1977, pp. 8-9).

I wonder then if that pessimism doesn't become a self fulfilling prophesy. For instance, I often wonder if the football team I assist doesn't lose games because it believes the other team is better. So it acts like an inferior team making fumbles, missing blocks, dropping passes, failing to tackle, or getting penalties at inopportune times.

Yet, I can't say that these teams won because I expected them to or their coaches expected they would either.

That may not be the point of the person-centered approach on this issue. (Cohen, 1994) may capture it though in writing, "Regardless of therapist orientation, clients perceived their therapists as helpful to the extent that they felt understood, cared for, and were respected for their own values and goals" (p. 6). A following quote from Rogers by Cohen though seems to indicate that this attitude does impact the therapy. "'. . .it is the way in which his attitudes and procedures are perceived which makes a difference to the client, and that it is this perception which is crucial' (Rogers, 1958, p. 9)" (p. 6).

Belief in the Potential of Persons

A basic premise of the approach can be stated as Callaghan (2008) wrote, "People are essentially trustworthy, vast potential for understanding selves, & resolving their own problems without direct intervention by therapist & are capable of self-directed growth if involved in a therapeutic relationship" (p. 6).

The "trustworthy" aspect may create some tension in light of the atrocities that human being commit against one another.

The resources are not presented here. They include personal psychological, community, and social, and I would also include spiritual resources.

In this I differ from Bozarth and other interpreters of the nondirective stance. I assert that the therapist is one of the resources. Withholding advice, information, or other resources available to the therapist assumes that these resources are worthless and of no value to the client who already has all the resources he or she needs for personal growth. I certainly agree that counselors and psychotherapists don't need to control, manipulate, or coerce clients into getting better, or in realizing their potential. But I also don't agree that advice or the sharing of knowledge is necessarily a violation of the approach. It may very well be that any given client doesn't have all the resources he or needs to make the changes he or she wants to. The therapist may have something the client can use. To withhold it in the name of being nondirective is itself presumptive.

I have come to see this trust in the client in relationship to the application or availability of the core conditions. Bozarth (2000) wrote that Rogers' theory "contends that this growth can be promoted by an individual perceiving certain conditions that are experienced by another individual (the therapist) towards her (the client). I will say this in a different way later, but the implicit practicality for therapy is that the individual must be free to follow her own way, in her own direction and at her own pace. It is the therapist/client relationship

and the resources of the client that are most important for success"
(pp. 27-28).

Acceptance of a wide range of human experiences

"The therapist must have no conditions of acceptance but must accept
and appreciate the client as is (Rogers, 1957). Hurtful, painful, bizarre,
and unusual feelings, as well as good feelings, are to be accepted by
the therapist. Acceptance does not mean agreement with the client
but rather refers to caring for the person as a separate individual"
(Sharf, 2000, p. 220).

The issue of unconditional positive regard has been dealt with in
another chapter. I consider it a mistake to call acceptance unconditional
positive regard. My concern with Sharf's description is the use of
the words "must" and "appreciate." Dr. Sharf may or may not be a
person-centered adherent in the Rogerian sense. That he picked up
on the legalism of the condition strikes me as important. For if the
approach is seen as legalistic, something has been miscommunicated.
In fact, Bozarth's (2000) work, at times, comes across to me as an
example of the legalism of the approach. The approach is about
liberation of the self and openness to the experiences of the person
(Rogers, 1977).

I have come to prefer the term undistracted acceptance. As I
indicated in the chapter on UPR, there are intense experiences of such
levels of concentration that the therapist can hear, sense, or grasp the
hurt, pain, feelings, and experiences of the client whether or not there
is positive regard. Positive regard may make it easier for the therapist
to be willing to receive the client's thoughts and experiences, but lack
of positive regard can be overcome with focus.

Of importance in this is that the client can tell the therapist
anything or withhold anything and not be charged with defensiveness
or manifesting some form of hostility. A ministerial colleague reported
to me that during his psychological evaluation for ordination he was
confronted with behavior about which he was unaware. When he
responded to the person who confronted him saying, "I never thought
about it that way," he was charged with being hostile and defensive.

This puzzled him since he felt he was being open to the observations of the psychologist evaluating him.

As a third party, I am not privy to the nonverbal communication that was being exuded from my colleague that may have triggered the psychologist's response. However, it does not matter. The response was radically different than the person-centered model. Confronting the allegedly defensiveness and hostility would have been different even if it was defensiveness and hostility. It would be received as part of the person's experience, with attempts to minimize any perceptions that the person ought not to have the feelings, or should do a better job of dealing with them.

The ethic here is acceptance of the client's experiences for what they are, regardless of how the therapist feels about them. Preference would be for the therapist to value the experiences of the client, but I have not found that is possible all the time or necessary all the time. Even the client fails to accept his or her own experiences all the time. That is part of the reason some come for therapy. They don't like what they experience and want to change it.

Can therapists be expected to like the client unconditionally when the client doesn't like him or her own self unconditionally? There are those who have asserted that unconditional positive regard is not a "liking" of the client. Personally it may be splitting hairs to make the distinction between prizing and liking.

Therefore I default to undistracted acceptance without the evaluation of whether it is unconditional positive regard or not.

Effort to understand the world of another

Obviously empathy is at the heart of this effort. There is a commitment to understanding the views, thoughts, and perspectives of the client. In this, there is no effort to say, "No, you really aren't experiencing such and such. You are really experiencing something else."

While I have concerns about the concept of unconditional positive regard, I don't about empathy. I consider holding fast to unconditional positive regard as possibly affirming antisocial and self-destructive behaviors. I can envision people believing that their behaviors are OK.

With empathy though, the therapist sees the behaviors, thoughts, experiences, and ideas in the clearest way. A person can't be helped if their experiences are not grasped and understood.

Empathy also is a compassionate response to grasping the world of the client. I can't think of a more compassionate way to help someone.

I have come to see therapy on three fronts: 1) The chance for a client to change his or her life. 2) Offering an easement from suffering. And 3) Engaging a person who is in such a state that there is no hope for any kind of change and the person has the right to be treated with dignity and respect in the midst of hopelessness or reality. Empathy, not the myth of unconditional positive regard, offers these possibilities.

Therefore, I consider the commitment to empathy as the premier ethical stance. Closely related to that is the effort to be empathic.

Makes no effort to manipulate or control others

I had four different therapists during my pilgrimage as a student seeking out therapy. Not one of them, each assuming a so-called directive position attempted to coerce or manipulate me.

Rogers (1977) seemed hypersensitive to that seeing the authoritarianism of other approaches such as psychoanalysis. Commenting on how the person-centered approach differs from other approaches Rogers wrote, "It as taken me years to recognize that the violent opposition to the client-centered therapy sprang not only from its newness, and the fact that it came from a psychologist rather than a psychiatrist, but primarily because it struck such an outrageous blow to the therapist's power" (p. 16).

I would submit while this may be true, what Rogers missed was how offensive his own assertions were. Rogers said again and again in various ways, "Politics, in the present-day psychological and social usage, has to do with power and control: with the extent to which persons desire, attempt to obtain, possess, share, or surrender power and control over others and/or themselves. It has to do with the maneuvers, the strategies and tactics, witting or unwitting, by which such power and control over one's own life and others' lives is sought and gained – or shared or relinquished. It has to do with the locus of decision-making power: who makes the decisions which, consciously or unconsciously, regulate or control the thoughts, feelings, or behavior of others or oneself" (p. 4). I am pretty sure that those who don't adhere to the person-centered approach sometimes are aghast that their commitment to diagnosis, treatment, cares plans, and psycho-social assessments are seen in such a poor light as to be considered unethical by the person-centered community. I have no reference for this position of such directive type approaches being seen as unethical save for numerous experiences at person-centered workshops where it is relatively safe to make such charges.

I have to admit that when I see coaches forcing football players to run hills for making a mistake that it stirs up my dismay at more directive responses to human behavior. Yet, forcing others to adopt more nondirective responses is also inappropriate.

This has led me to reject the concept of being nondirective. If the approach coerces people to adopt the nondirective stance, even via peer pressure, I can't see how it can be called nondirective. It still is pulling power plays over others.

Pulling power-plays defies the ethics of the approach.

A Commitment to the Core Conditions

The issue of power over others seems like an inadequate place to end a chapter on person-centered ethics. So, I leave it restating that the ethics of the approach are captured in a commitment to adhering to, or offering the core conditions of acceptance, empathy, and genuineness.

Bozarth (2000) as much as I disagree with his insistence that person-centered therapists adhere to a Rogerian understanding of the approach, and that people who differ simply misunderstand Rogers, seems to me to highlight that the core conditions are intertwined. That when one is genuinely empathic, one has unconditional positive regard for the client. They all go together.

I don't accept that fully. That is, I might on any given occasion genuinely not understand while trying to understand. That might be good enough in this moment. I might be genuinely negative in my regard. How, I deal with that is important. If I mistreat a client, that is flat out unethical. If I recognize my negative regard, and channel my energy to recognizing rather than denying that negative regard, and channel my energy towards understanding the client, I have not violated the client. Thus, I assert that acceptance might be different in any moment from empathy. Acceptance is possible when I don't understand.

And finally, I can say that the genuine therapist may not be positive, or understanding in any given moment. The client surely isn't either. To see that the therapist also is not might indeed by growthful. It says, "I the client don't have to positive all the time, or negative all the time."

I have tended to believe my person-centered colleagues tend not to trust the following comments by Rogers (1957b) very much regarding the genuine/congruent therapist:

It means that with the relationship he is freely and deeply himself, with his actually experience accurately represented by his awareness of himself. It is the opposite of presenting a facade, either knowingly or unknowingly.

It is necessary (nor is it possible) that the therapist be a paragon who exhibits this degree of integration, of wholeness, in every aspect of his life. It is sufficient that he is accurately himself in this hour of this relationship, that in this basic sense he is what he actually is, in this moment of time.

It should be clear that includes being himself even in ways which are not regarded as ideal for psychotherapy. His experience may be 'I am afraid of this client' or 'My attention is so focused on my own problems that I can scarcely listen to him.' If the therapist is not denying these feelings to awareness, but is able freely to be them (as well as being his other feelings), then the condition we have stated is met.

It would take us too far afield to consider the puzzling matter as to the degree to which the therapist overtly communicates this reality in himself to the client. Certainly the aim is not for the therapist to express or talk out his own feelings, but primarily that he should not be deceiving the client as to himself. At times he may need to talk out some of his own feelings (either to the client, or to a colleague or supervisor) if they are standing in the way . . ." (p. 224) of empathy and acceptance.

I also find myself wondering often if those experiences and feelings of the therapist don't say a great deal about the feelings and experiences of the clients. Sharing them might open doors for exploration, or gets the therapist back on track with the client if the therapist is in error.

Very importantly, the position on genuineness is not permission to violate ethical, moral, or legal standards.

Nor are the other conditions a basis for coercing a therapist to be more empathic or accepting.

Rather, it about a spontaneous "way of being" (Rogers, 1980).

Laissez Faire

This last section is my stuff. I find no support for it in the literature. I would suspect there would be a denial of my position in the person-centered community.

It is related to the appearance of condoning all sorts of previously regarded antisocial behavior in the name of sustaining unconditional positive regard.

I remember a person being brought to a person-centered workshop who was planning on having a sex change operation. There were no questions. There was no open questioning of the person's experience.

The young woman was a construction worker. She allegedly wore a binding that flattened her chest concealing her breasts. She spoke in a deep rough voice in the stereo-typical manner of macho-men construction workers.

However, she often circulated around the community meetings asking people if they needed anything. A feminine side kept emerging. Certainly men have such feminine qualities. And I may have taken more notice of the famine side of her body language and her behavior because I had been told that she was a female.

That aside, I didn't hear anyone wonder out loud, and that included me, about the long term medical consequences of surgically constructed male sex organs. I didn't hear anyone point out how feminine her behavior was and how incongruent it was with being a male construction worker.

What I heard was keep your mouth shut. Don't ask questions that appear to be judgmental. You'll be ganged up on by the community for being judgmental about this situation.

One is not wonder aloud in the person-centered community about homosexuality and abortion. Taking a stance of believing that homosexuality and abortion are moral issues is judgmental. Taking a stance on condemning religion, or wondering out loud about these issues are considered judgmental.

There seems to be a double standard. Don't be judgmental about heretofore behaviors that were not condoned by society, but kick butt if someone fails to overtly condone those behaviors. They are being judgmental and intolerant.

I wonder if that has not contributed to the failure of the world in general, the religious community in general, and some aspects of the psychotherapeutic community in particular to embrace the approach.

It may very well be that tolerating or condoning all behaviors in the name of unconditional positive regard, or nonjudgmentalness, is not acceptable in society. Thus, the approach is not generally acceptable, appearing too tolerant and anarchical.

I remember a colleague saying that she believed that it was OK to smoke marijuana, have open sexual experiences, drink heavily, and other behaviors in the person-centered community. She stated she didn't appreciate the judgmentalness that might inhibit these behaviors, especially in the person-centered community.

It gave me some hope that the community has principles that not just any behavior was acceptable.

So there perhaps, even in my concerns, is my myth of laissez faire. The person-centered approach may not really condone everything. Perhaps as Sharf (2000) indicated the approach does not condone socially unacceptable behavior. Though there is some willingness to redescribe or redefine socially unacceptable behavior.

I rather like the idea of the community making decisions about these issues rather than some institution. Yet, all institutions exist because of communities and often reflect the values of those communities.

There is then some tension regarding this person-centered approach which attempts to be respectful of the potentials of persons as those potentials conflict with the interests of others. Thus, institutions form, protecting common interests and attempt to get others to conform or behave properly.

Could it be that the informal person-centered community is also a community that has ethical principles that it expects its adherents to accept? There may not be an officially designated group of people to judge the violators. There may be on any given occasion self appointed people who make those judgments.

These though seem to me more consistent with the approach than the concept of nonjudgmentalness. In fact, there is judgmentalness in the adherents to the approach even if it is only seen in being judgmental about nonjudgmentalness.

Adherents to the approach are expected to have ethical principles consistent with the approach, but there is no formal institution to enforce them.

References

Bozarth, J. D. (2000). Forty years of dialogue with Rogers' hypothesis. In D. Bower (Ed.), *The person-centered approach: applications for living.* New York: Writers Club Press, 27-54.

Callaghan, G. M. (2008). *Methods of psychotherapy: Person-centered therapy,* PSYC 258, San José State University. http://psych.sjsu.edu/~glennc/courses/psy258/index.html

Cohen, J. (1994). Empathy toward client perception of therapist intent: Evaluating one's person-centeredness. *The Person-Centered Journal.* 1(3), 4-10.

ethics. (n.d.). Dictionary.com Unabridged (v 1.1). Retrieved February 18, 2008, from Dictionary.com website: http://dictionary.reference.com/browse/ethics

Report of the Ethics Committee. (2006). *American Psychologist.* 62(5) , 504-511.

Rogers. C. R. (1957a). A note on "the nature of man." Reprinted in H. Kirschenbaum, & V. L. Henderson (Eds.). *The Carl Rogers reader* (1989). Boston. Houghton Mifflin, 401- 408.

Rogers. C. R. (1957b). The necessary and sufficient conditions of therapeutic personality change. Reprinted in H. Kirschenbaum, & V. L. Henderson (Eds.). *The Carl Rogers reader* (1989). Boston. Houghton Mifflin, 219-235.

Rogers, C. R. (1961). *On becoming a person.* Boston: Houghton Mifflin.

Rogers. C. R. (1977). *On personal power: Inner strength and its revolutionary impact.* New York: A Delta Book.

Rogers, C. R. (1980). *A way of being.* Boston: Houghton Mifflin.

Sharf, R. S. (2000). *Theories of psychotherapy & counseling: Concepts and cases.* Belmont, CA: Brooks/Cole.

Title 43. (2007). Professions and businesses. Chapter 10a: Professional counselors, social workers, and marriage and family therapists Georgia Code, the State of Georgia, O.C.G.A. § 43-10A

On A Person-Centered Religion:

Doug Bower's Partial Christian Perspective

This chapter did not capture thoughts I had in contemplating writing it. As it unfolded, it turned out differently than I thought it would. If I should write on the theme again, it might offer different slants than it does now. I simply let it evolve for what it became.

A Belief in God

I find no contradiction in having faith and believing in the potentials of a person called a client. I had faith before I discovered the person-centered approach. I found no overt effort to discourage my faith. However, I did find objections towards espousing positions based on my faith in person-centered communities. I suppose that can be interpreted as discouragement to have or present faith. I do not attribute those objections to the person-centered approach's positions. The objections are common in the conflict of secular - sacred dialogues that have occurred throughout the centuries. They have been around for some time and were even articulated in Berkhof (1941). Rogers isn't mentioned at all. A significant work of some importance (1942) obviously wasn't even prepared and wasn't about faith anyway. Thus, issues raised about spirituality and/or faith are not related to the person-centered approach itself.

I can't say the opposite either. The person-centered approach gave me no grounds for having faith either. The approach isn't about encouraging the development of faith. It is about grasping the world as others see it.

However, I will attempt latter to get at some principles that I thought allowed me to grow in my faith. For now, here are some brief additional assertions concerning my faith in relationship to being person-centered.

In The Image of God

It is real clear that the Genesis account makes at least two points. First, that human beings are created in the image of God. "So God created man in his own image, in the image of God created he him; male and female created he them" Genesis 1:27 (KJV). What that means is far too broad to struggle with here. Yet, it seems that such a position is congruent with the person-centered assertion, that people have vast personal resources for personal growth. Adams (1979) discards this claim since the claim implies that people already have everything they need to be whole. Personally, I think Adams both misses the mark and offers a corrective for the nondirective position. The Rogerian position of self actualization is a constantly changing process. Thus, it is not a process whereby a person has every thing needed for growth. However, making adjustments and assimilating new experiences to enhance the person's directions is an important component of self-actualization. The Rogerian model trusts that process and is concerned about some "expert" making assumptions that will thwart that process rather than liberate it.

Adams corrective touches on the theme of not having all the resources one needs from the beginning of life. I personally see that while the client has vast resources for personal growth, if he or she comes to me, the client deliberately adds another person to those vast resources. To then deny the client access to those new resources found in the therapist thwarts the client's efforts to change. A rigid commitment to being nondirective which sees overtly advising, guiding, suggesting, prescribing, etc., is unethical or a violation of the approach stiff arms the client's efforts to seek ways to change. It keeps new ideas from the client and prevents the client from deciding which of these ideas could work or not work. The therapist thus decides that his or her ideas violate the client's autonomy instead of the client making that decision.

Second, the Rogerian position holds that human beings were created good. Not too surprisingly, Jay Adams discards Carl Rogers' claim, that human beings are basically good. Rogers (1986) certainly acknowledged that his optimistic claim was part of what made his theory and practice different from psychoanalysis and Christian positions.

When I began exploring the person-centered approach, I felt my view that human beings were sinners came in conflict with the traditional Rogerian position. I even made a concerted effort to abandon that position. However, reading, and seeing report after report of humanity's inhumanity towards fellow human beings hindered my complete movement towards such an optimistic position. Even though Rogers asserted that his position was not some Pollyannaish stance was in denial of the atrocities committed by human beings, the emphasis on the goodness of human beings did indeed feel like denial. If all it takes to get people to be more humane are three basic conditions, one has to give a far deeper accounting of why that doesn't happen than the person-centered approach does. Being concerned that the core conditions are not readily manifested in society doesn't get at what is behind their not being manifested in society.

Later, I came to believe that a commitment to the core conditions was essential, not a belief in the goodness of human beings. Such a belief would be yet another condition necessary for therapy. Actually, I see no evidence that anyone even needs to have such a positive belief in order to make a commitment to empathy, acceptance, and genuineness.

Thus, I found that I can still believe people are sinners in need of God's love and redemption, and still be committed to the core conditions. I don't see that this hinders my ability to offer the core conditions.

However, even if I held that human beings are basically good, that still is consistent with the Genesis account. On the day that human beings were created the Genesis account says, "And God saw every thing that he had made, and, behold, it was very good. And the evening and the morning were the sixth day" Genesis 1:31

(KJV). There is no indication, as the Calvinists, say that people are so deprived that the divine spark associated with being made in the image of God has disappeared because of sin. Therefore, Adams' (1979) assertion is an over reaction to the optimism of the person-centered approach.

In a conversation with a person-centered colleague, we essentially agreed that people are basically good and evil. I assert that using the core conditions tends to bring out the positive elements of what it means for this particular client to be a person.

Belief in God's Creature: The Human Being

Essentially, my person-centered position stands in awe of what people can do in the face of great adversity. Rogers' (1980) potato illustration was in part a metaphor concerning those people in the old back wards of mental hospitals that somehow survived. In my practice, I am often amazed at how people overcame problems often very quickly following being in a place where they and I had given up hope that the problem could be fixed.

I do not see that as being foreign to or against the awe of faith. "When I consider thy heavens, the work of thy fingers, the moon and the stars, which thou hast ordained; What is man, that thou art mindful of him? and the son of man, that thou visitest him? For thou hast made him a little lower than the angels, and hast crowned him with glory and honour" Psalm 8:3-5 (KJV). Such a statement gets lost in a traditional Christian model that asserts that human beings are sinners who deserve condemnation. Of course, focusing on the goodness of human beings denies the sinful nature of human beings and its trappings. Such awe in the person-centered approach and the perspective of my Christian faith feel compatible.

A Rediscovery of Scripture

An important part of my Christian pilgrimage has been my interaction with the Old and New Testaments. I found a couple principles of the person-centered approach that enhanced by encounters with Scripture.

First, people can be trusted. They can be trusted to speak to their experiences. They can be trusted to make decisions that will enhance their lives. It is distrust that fosters untrustworthiness in people.

I took this premise into my Bible studies. In 1977, I began reading the Bible from beginning to end during the course of the year. I have continued to do so every year.

I make a concerted effort to grasp the writings as if I am the writer. I began doing that sometime in the early eighties.

Prior to that, my readings were cloudy. I had been influenced by the historical-critical methodologies. These methodologies hardly confirmed the materials of scripture. They seemed far more laced with doubt and skepticism. They certainly were external expert oriented methodologies that discarded the content of Scripture. In these approaches, there is no creation, no exodus event. The existence of King David is doubtful. There is no virgin birth, and there is no resurrection of Jesus. Matthew didn't write Matthew. Mark didn't write Mark. Luke didn't write Luke. John didn't write all of John and other writings attributed to him. Paul wrote most of that which was attributed to him. There really isn't much left to believe.

Under the premise of trusting persons to present their world view, I came to have a greater appreciation for the presentation of the Biblical writers of their faith view.

Second, the premise of empathy was important in my pilgrimage with Scripture. In approaching the writings empathically, I came away feeling that the writers of the Old Testament and the New Testament absolutely positively believed what they were writing. If they can be trusted as much as anyone else can to describe their experiences, they attempted to describe their experiences and observations concerning what they believed of God.

The above position is a whole lot different than believing that Scripture is simply a collection of myths and legends not to be taken seriously. Believing that the Scripture was written by people who were doing their best to describe events, circumstances, and experiences concerning God's interaction with human beings is a different place than dismissing those writings.

The Person-Centered Approach and Pastoral Care/Counseling

(Hiltner, 1949; Oates, 1974; Holifield 1983; Clinebell, 1984; Wicks, Parsons, & Capps, 1985) among many others affirmed the influence Rogers and the person-centered approach on pastoral care and pastoral counseling. This did not mean that pastoral care givers and counselors claimed to become person-centered as a whole. There were indeed a wide range of influences even on the above contributors.

I personally did and have asserted that I became person-centered. However, I can't say that I became Rogerian. I think I have demonstrated that purposefully and nonpurposefully throughout this present work. I am far more interested in the person being true to one's self. If that matches up well with what Rogers presented as the heart of this approach, great. I am not, however, prepared to say that those who match-up well with Rogers are Rogerians.

I will not deny that there are those who have appeared to me to have made themselves into Rogerians, but my experience is that such persons take offense to being accused of becoming Rogerian clones.

I am interested though in what makes the approach a good theory and practice for pastoral care and counseling. I would offer the following without explanation. A commitment to the core conditions and their implementation seems to me to be very compatible with "doing onto others as you would have them do unto you." This commitment seems equally compatible to offering care to those who are sick and afflicted. "Bear ye one another's burdens, and so fulfil the law of Christ" Galatians 6:2 (KJV).

Also the emphasis on nonjudgmentalness appears to be compatible with Biblical themes. "Judge not, that ye be not judged" Matthew 7:1 (KJV). This may come across as legalistic. However, the person-centered approach to this doesn't come across to me any less so. So much so that I have rejected it as a premise of the approach since it is not practiced and growth still occurs anyway. Yet, that nonjudgmentalness is part of the person-centered approach and the Christian faith may not be as coincidental as it might seem. Rogers was raised in a fundamentalist family which appeared from my readings to be Reformed or Calvinistic in theology (Kirschenbaum, 1979).

Then, lastly, I emphasized above a belief in persons. I certainly feel that people being made in the "image of God" means there are inner and outer resources for personal growth and change ingrained in and available to individuals. Such a position may not be essential to being person-centered, but it is compatible with the secular version of the approach.

Away From Legalism and Authoritarianism

Finally, the ideal of this approach to me as a believer is a movement away from legalism. "But Jesus called them to Himself and said, 'You know that the rulers of the Gentiles lord it over them, and their great men exercise authority over them. It is not this way among you, but whoever wishes to become great among you shall be your servant, and whoever wishes to be first among you shall be your slave; just as the Son of Man did not come to be served, but to serve, and to give His life a ransom for many'" Matthew 20:25-28 (NASB).

Christian history is replete with power-plays, manipulation, exercising control over others through various Church leaders and Church institutions. I have had several power-plays pulled on me through the years which, had I not acquiesced to, I would not have even been ordained. One power-play was having to take the MMPI through a center designated by the Conference as if going to any well trained psychologist was not worthy of consideration. Actually to take that instrument at all to get ordained is loaded with problems. I didn't know that at the time. It isn't an instrument of determining valid candidates for ministry. Further, its emphasis on pathology means that people who have no business seeing a person's pathology and can't do anything about it anyway get to see that pathology. The requirement to take the MMPI is about hoop jumping. While a little power-play in the scheme of things, it still is a power-play. I wonder how the apostles would have fared on the MMPI.

The theme here is about facilitation, not authoritarianism and legalism. Bower (1985) spoke to the Christian pastoral counselor giving up institutional authority to empower individuals to explore, discover, and speak about their personal worlds. This attitude drops assumptions about the client's perspective. It asks, how can I as a therapist/counselor help you get at your experiences, thoughts, and ideas. This approach appears to me to be less likely to trigger defense mechanisms and have more respect for defense mechanisms when they occur than the other models I have observed. I find no help in being distracted by complexes, defenses, and alleged transferences and counter-transferences. They seem authoritarian and legalistic to me by virtue of the assumptions about clients. They are based on the learning of the therapist/counselor rather than the world view of the client. Empathy, acceptance, and congruence feel far more open to the experience of the other person who is before me. I can't think of anything more pastoral than that.

Finale'

This articulation feels inadequate of my ongoing and constantly changing positions. I have addressed it better in my own mind than I have in writing. It will have to do for now.

References

Adams, J. (1979). *A theology of Christian counseling.* Grand Rapids, Michigan: Zondervan Publishing House.

Berkhof, L. (1941). *Systematic theology.* Grand Rapids, Michigan: Wm. B. Eerdmans Publishing Co.

Bower, D. W. (1985). *Assumptions and attitudes of the Rogerian person-centered approach to counseling: Implications for pastoral counseling.* Unpublished graduate project. Columbia Theological Seminary.

Clinebell, H. (1984). *Basic types of pastoral care & counseling: Resources for the ministry of healing & growth.* Nashville: Abingdon Press.

Hiltner, S. (1949). *Pastoral counseling: How every pastor can help people to help themselves.* Nashville: Abingdon Press.

Holifield, E. B. (1983). *A history of pastoral care in American: From salvation to self-realization.* Nashville, Abingdon Press.

Kirschenbaum, H. (1979). *On becoming Carl Rogers.* New York: Delta Press.

Oates, W. E. (1974). *Pastoral counseling.* Philadelphia: Westminster Press.

Rogers, C. R. (1980). *A way of being.* Boston: Houghton Mifflin.

Rogers, C. R. (1986). Rogers, Kohut, and Erickson: A personal perspective on some similarities and differences. *Person-Centered Review* 1(2), 125-140.

Wicks, R. J., Parsons, R. D., & Capps, D. E. (Eds.) (1985). *Clinical handbook of pastoral counseling.* New York: Integration Books.

A Criticism of the Person-Centered Approach Of Carl Rogers

Having spent 27 years investigating, exploring and struggling with the Person-Centered theory of Carl Rogers, I have felt that Rogers and his disciples have not been very self critical. This is understandable in that Rogers was attempting to articulate his discoveries and their validity and not trying to provide his critics with ammunition or do their work for them.

I have noticed also that critical statements about the theory have tended to verge on being pot-shots rather than carefully thought out reactions which come from understanding Rogers' theory. So it is the purpose of this chapter to bring together criticisms as well as raise my own criticism of the Person-Centered Approach. The chapter is not a rejection of the approach, or an effort to provide ammunition for rejection of the theory. The paper is being written to provoke thoughtful criticism. The reader obviously would be the person doing the thoughtful part which might lead to the conclusion that this effort was languid at best or sloppy at worst. On the other hand perhaps, the effort here will be celebrated and appreciated.

I am approaching my criticism as a licensed professional counselor who had aspirations of becoming a formal pastoral counselor. I abandoned the formal seeking of officially becoming a pastoral counselor when I found that I regarded this approach as being pastoral. I also found I wasn't willing to take formal steps to get recognition as a pastoral counselor.

I am sold on the validity of the approach. I did not have any training with Carl Rogers, though I did exchange letters with him shortly before his death. I might have been more aggressive about communicating with Carl Rogers. However, I was receiving negative reports about his health. I felt I would be a burden. If I had to do it over again, I would make a stronger attempt to communicate with Carl Rogers and let him decide if he wanted to communicate rather than let others discourage me from my efforts. My own letter to him is now lost as I stored it on an early desktop floppy disk. I upgraded my pc to an IBM. A few years later I tossed out the old floppy disks not thinking about the letter which was stored on the desk. Fortunately, I do have Rogers' response to my letter on file.

I do not regard the theory as sacred or infallible. And I am not a purist. I don't consider myself a Rogerian, but a Bowerian. I simply found that qualities that I have long held, which Rogers (1980) and others called "core conditions" where regarded as therapeutic. I approach the Person-Centered Approach feeling that I am free from the restraints of being Rogerian. Being free of influence and training from the formative years of the approach should allow me to hear and accept the criticisms of the theory. This is not always true as I have often defended and explained the position to peers and other professionals who have questioned the value and validity of the theory. My belief that I may be free to hear and accept the criticisms of the approach may be delusional, but it is my delusion.

In my first formal exposure to the PCA taking Jerold Bozarth's in his Person-Centered course on counseling and psychotherapy, as well as his counseling practicum at the University of Georgia, Bozarth spoke of a trip to London for the second annual Person-Centered convention. He said that he was accused of being liberal with his views concerning empathic responses. He stated that there is a faction of Person-Centered theorists who rigidly follow the theory. If this is or was the case, I believe they fail to hear legitimate criticism without providing explanation for and about the theory in relationship to criticism. I certainly believe the theory has been well presented without criticism. However, self-criticism or openness to the criticism of others seems important to me. I believe that openness is lost in defensiveness about criticism.

My search for criticism began as I noticed that Rogers and others spent a great deal of time presenting the results of findings which supported his attitudinal principles of empathy, unconditional positive regard and congruence as they related to the core presupposition of self actualization. I tend to be suspicious that the instruments were slanted toward the Person-Centered theory by the mere fact the jargon of the instruments seemed to be Person-Centered jargon. Over the years, I have become even more skeptical about the validity and the reliability of appropriate instruments regarding the approach. So much so, that I don't believe there is an instrument to determine that positive regard can be determined to be unconditional. This in turn impacts the "necessary and sufficient conditions" espoused by Rogers (1957). In dealing with existing instruments, clients and observers were/are limited to the use of the jargon used to describe therapy or their experiences with Person-Centered therapy. Thus they might have substantiated that, when the attitudinal principles were in place during therapy, the client would be more self actualizing. They also would have to deal with the terms commonly surrounding the "core conditions" (Rogers, 1961, 1980). To date I have not seen any material which confirms or denies my suspicions. Jerold Bozarth pointed me to (Garfield & Bergin, 1986) and (Gurman & Razin, 1977). However, I was less than convinced concerning upr and the conditions being "necessary and sufficient." I am very convinced the PCA is at least as effective as any other approach to healing or psychotherapy is. In my search, I have yet to directly see the instruments which were used to allegedly confirm the Rogerian theory. Thus, my suspicions still remain.

This suspicion did start me on a search. I very early in my exposure to the PCA started asking professors and practitioners of psychotherapy what criticisms they had. I was often disappointed by what I heard not because the truth hurt, but because the initial responses to my seeking critical statements about the Person-Centered approach tended to be superficial and seemed to come out of misunderstandings of the theory rather than thoughtful interaction with the theory. Bozarth (1998) indicates a profound awareness of these misunderstandings and is critical of them.

On one occasion I received an unsolicited criticism. I was awaiting supervision and reading Rogers' "On Personal Power" when one of the therapists at the center sarcastically said, "Rogers doesn't have any personal power." It was clearly a pot-shot and reflected the struggle regarding the approach in relationship to other approaches. Is personal power being able to tell people off? Is it being able to stand up for what you believe? Is it being able to solve other people's problems by telling them what they should do? Is it being able to give up one's authoritarian position and grasp an authority which allows the other person to discover self authority? Rogers view is clearly the latter (Rogers, 1977). It is has been my own discovery that it takes a great deal of personal power to give up authority. The therapist's statement came not out an understanding of Rogers but came out of biased position which is in a different paradigm than Rogers' position.

One another occasion I asked my therapist if he had a criticism of the Person-Centered theory. He shared a joke about a suicidal patient and his Person-Centered therapist:

C1: "I feel like I want to commit suicide."

T1: "You feel like you want to commit suicide."

C2: "I think I'll jump out the window." The client moves to the window.

T2: "You think you'll jump out the window." The therapist moves to the window.

C3: "I am going to jump." The client jumps. Plop!

T3: "You're going to jump." The therapist looks out the window and says, "Plop."

This criticism came out of the common reaction to the notion that reflection is the chief technique in the Person-Centered approach in conducting therapy. And although "Temaner believes that in developing a relationship with a client there is no other way then through a process of interaction in which the therapist expresses reflections . . ." (Bozarth & Temaner, 1984, pp. 7-8), I believe this is a gross distraction in the field. Reflection is not the key to empathy. There is no key response in empathy (Bozarth, 1984). The only key to empathy is to do whatever is necessary to enter into, to perceive and to understand the world of the client.

Further, although Carl Rogers does indeed tend to be reflective, he does not use reflection in the way some human relations people do. That is, he does not tend to just repeat the last thing the client says. In fact he wrote unfavorably about this kind of reflection himself.

"This tendency to focus on the therapist's responses had appalling consequences. I had met hostility, but these reactions were worse. The whole approach came, in a few years, to be known as a technique. 'Nondirective therapy, it was said, 'is the technique of reflecting the client's feelings.' Or an even worse caricature was simply that 'in nondirective therapy you repeat the last words the client has said. I was so shocked by these distortions of our approach that for a number of years I said almost nothing about empathic listening . . ." (Rogers, 1980, p. 139).

The focus of this criticism of the Rogerian approach was directed toward the technique of reflection and not upon the underlying theory. Personally, I found the technique of reflection useful as a novice, but for a maturing therapist it lacks personal impact. I find that I still tend to use reflection not when I am being empathic but when I am having difficulty understanding. I also tend to use it when what the client is saying is so obvious that it leaps out at me and I spontaneously repeat what the client says.

There are a couple of my own criticisms for which I have not found written support concerning reflection. The first is that I personally believe that it is an insult to the client. The client usually knows what has been said and does not need someone to repeat it. It sounds patronizing. I write this even though just saying above that I do repeat what the client says.

The second is that just because a therapist is reflecting does not mean that the therapist has an adequate understanding at all. He or she may actually be misunderstanding and blocking empathy by assuming that a reflective response adequately conveys that the therapist understands when in actuality the therapist may have no idea what the client means by a word or phrase.

The third criticism I have is that reflection sounds so mechanical. When I hear people use it, I feel embarrassed. It doesn't sound like an interaction. I am aware that I have experienced it as insulting of people (patronizing) by the use of the technique in daily interactions. It seems often that reflection becomes a technique to be used in a mechanical way to avoid encountering another person in a significant way.

Related to these criticisms on reflection is another criticism which is directed more toward the theory as a whole as well as its practice. Howard J. Clinebell, Jr. (1966), Professor of pastoral counseling at the School of Theology at Claremont, California, accused the Person-Centered approach of being passive. He wrote (1966), "The pastor sees many troubled people who lack the ability to respond to the relatively passive Rogerian approach. It must be modified in a more active direction if they are to receive help" (p. 30).

It seems that Dr. Clinebell believed that the Rogerian theory and certainly its practice is one of inactivity. The therapist must seem to sit on his derriere' and not participate. This would seem to advocate passivity.

However, the theory and its use are anything but passive. It takes a great deal of effort to enter the world of the client.

It takes a great deal of self discipline to prevent one's impatience from interfering with the client's growth. It takes a great deal of personal power to have faith that the client is a self actualizing individual who has the capacity to move in a self directive way.

Outwardly, this may indeed appear to be a passive theory. However, inwardly and usually outwardly, the therapist's activity can be seen. If one watches Rogers at work in the films he has made of therapeutic sessions, one can see that he is anything but inactive. The problem usually arises because of impatience and the desire to solve a client's problem for the client. The critics want to do something or say something profound which will move the client toward healing. They feel helpless if they don't.

Another criticism from Clinebell is that the Person-Centered approach is antiauthoritarian. Clinebell argues that persons who are trained in the Person-Centered approach are discouraged in using their personal authority to deal with clients. "The Rogerian model has tended to make the minister feel that he should strenuously avoid the use of his authority - i.e. he should not advise, direct, inspire, or teach in his counseling relationships" (p. 30).

My own tendency is to support this. The practitioner is discouraged from using directive skills, skills which may have developed through years of struggling with authority and the carving out of one's own authority in the College of Hard Knocks. The theory clearly argues that being directive is not valuable to the client. In my own personal growth I found confrontation by authoritarian practitioners very helpful. I learned to stand up on my own two feet and not get blown away by these folks. I didn't like it because it often hurt to deal with my insecurities and lack of confidence in myself, but I was able to grow through being confronted in some seemingly arrogant and hostile ways. However, the Person-Centered approach was even more helpful to me in this regard than anything I previously encountered.

The Person-Centered idea is that therapist is taking on a new directive style. It is the style of being self directive and the thus allowing the client to become more self directive in as much at it may be possible for that individual. The Person-Centered approach thus offers a new paradigm of authority which denies that telling others who they are, what they can do and how they can do it. The Person-Centered theory holds that authoritarianism results from incongruence marked by impatience, lack of faith in the self actualization process and anxiety. True authority in this approach rests in being congruent; being able to empathize and accept others no matter how different they are from the therapist.

Another criticism is that the therapy of the Person-Centered approach is not effective for everyone. One of the first issues that my pastoral counseling supervisor at the Atlanta Psychiatric Clinic, raised was whether I believed that there were clients with which the Person-Centered approach would not work. I stated that I could not envision any situation that the basic attitudinal principles could not be used. A peer of mine at the University of Georgia stated that he could not see how the Person-Centered approach could work for schizophrenics or others with radical pathology. Rogers himself and his followers apparently noted that there was no significant measurable improvement in the schizophrenics he worked with in Wisconsin as compared to control groups. Lewis R. Wolberg (1977) stated, "Client-centered methods are most useful in individuals of relatively sound personality structure who require aid in clarifying their ideas about a current life difficulty" (p. 124).

The key word is work. The theory does not "work" for anybody. It trusts that within the individual is the capacity to move in a self directive way. The approach is not supposed to "work." It is supposed to maximize the self actualization tendencies, tendencies which will be at work in one form or another no matter what is happening in the client's life. "To be a client-centered therapist is to risk relinquishing the props provided by degrees, graduate training, and technique and instead to meet the client as a person, to be of service in an authentic relationship that has yet to take shape" (Raskin, Rogers, & Witty, 2008, p. 141). The problem rests in not trusting self actualization enough to look at what is different about the client and seeing that difference as evidence of self actualization. Our measurements through various instruments of testing may not be prepared to deal with these kinds of changes in schizophrenic states. And thus we may not be able to measure the fine changes which occur in self actualizing persons.

Yet another criticism is that the Rogerian theory does not focus on the unconscious. Hall and Lindzey (1978) stated, "We find theories such as Allport's, Lewin's, Goldstein's, Skinner's, Rogers', and existentialism where unconscious motives are de-emphasized or ceded an unimportant role" (p. 683). One does not have to look far in Rogers' works to see that this is true. He did deny the unconscious. He just did not believe people act out the past in unconscious ways.

This criticism is up for grabs depending on one's theoretical orientation. I personally have had some difficulty thinking of unconscious processes. I have tended not to like thinking in terms of my own unconscious motives. However, I have often enjoyed noticing unconscious motives behind the behavior of others. I do not believe that a therapist should use these as a club to convince the client that his/her problem is the result of mismanagement at the oral stage, etc. At some level it makes sense that due to the whole make up of human beings that the present (the here and now) of the baby will affect the future of that person as it develops. Thus, when that baby turns thirty, his life beginnings may have an effect on him or her.

Further, the Person-Centered argument diminishing the value of the unconscious doesn't focus on the unconscious physiological mechanisms that influence behavior which can never be made conscious, i.e., low blood sugar, thyroid malfunctions, etc. It has been well documented that our bodies can and do affect behavior. These effects arise unconsciously and often manifest themselves in conscious behavior for which there seems to be no understandable rational to the person enduring the behavior, i.e., low blood sugar can cause depression and irritability and the patient cannot explain why he or she feels these emotions.

Another criticism is that in spite of arguing against determinism in the human experience through unconscious motives, the Person-Centered approach still tends to be deterministic because of its emphasis on a phenomenological view. This point is argued by C.H. Patterson (1966): "Phenomenology assumes that although a real world may exist, its existence cannot be known or experienced directly. Its existence is inferred on the basis of perceptions of the world. These perceptions constitute the phenomenal field, or the phenomenal world, of the individual. Man can know only his phenomenal world, never any real world. Therefore, he can only behave in terms of how he perceived things, or how they appear to him" (p. 432).

Patterson states that this phenomenology is deterministic. The person must behave in accordance to this perceived world.

According to Patterson, Rogers recognizes self direction and choice as within the self. However, he argues that Rogers fails to recognize "the conflict between the assumptions of phenomenology and his system . . . but he does recognize the difference between the determinism of science and the assumption of his system" (p. 434).

To be honest, I have difficulty understanding this criticism. It might be related to a statement that Jerold Bozarth often makes to classes and workshops, "The client is always doing the best he can do." Is there determinism in believing this?

My own criticism of this would be to say that it appears to contradict the notions of self direction and choice. If these are actualities in the person's life, then it may be quite possible that a person may not always do the best he can do by choosing not to do the best he can do. Further, to say that the client is doing the best he can do implies that the person has no other options. So the pyromaniac can only be a pyromaniac. The child molester can only be a child molester. Given their phenomenological fields, these people will continue to light fires or molest children. The therapist then has to become resigned and passive as Clinebell argued and accept the fact that the pyromaniac is a pyromaniac and that there is nothing which can be done about it.

However, this determinism comes in conflict with Rogers' (1951) observations of the changes that clients report as therapy progresses. He states that:

> ". . . 1) During the latter part of therapy the client's conversation includes an increased discussion of plans and behavioral steps to be undertaken, and discussion of the outcomes of these steps.
>
> ". . . 2) in successful client-centered therapy, an examination of all references to current behavior indicates that there is a change from relatively immature behavior to relatively mature behavior during the course of the interviews.
>
> ". . . 3) . . . there is a decrease in psychological tension as evidenced in the client's verbal productions.
>
> ". . . 4) . . . there appears to be a decrease in current defensive behaviors and a greater awareness of those defensive behaviors which are present.
>
> ". . . 5) . . . the client shows an increased tolerance for frustration as objectively measured in physiological terms.
>
> ". . . 6) one behavioral outcome . . . is improved functioning in life tasks . . ." (pp. 180-185).

It is clear here that Rogers argues for change. This change seems to take place within the phenomenological field as the client begins to perceive him/her self and the world in a different manner. Thus, the approach is not a locked determinism stating the person will only act in accordance to the way he or she perceives the self and never change. The person is always changing in one way or another and the pyromaniac may have the capacity to stop being a pyromaniac provided the real world a-round the self is perceived and experienced in a different way.

The last criticism of the Person-Centered theory has to do with the absence of a notion of self destruction within the person. It seems quite difficult to just see human beings as basically self actualizing and good in light of war, murder, rape, theft, oppression, prejudice, deception, mental illness and even death. There is no room for evil in Rogers' model. There is no acknowledgment of sin as with Menninger (1973). Thus, there is no concept of self destruction in spite of tremendous evidence to the contrary as with Fromm (1973).

This self destructive tendency can be seen in this following illustration. It is well known that some babies get diaper rash. At first this rash is evidence of self actualization. Blood vessels in the perineal area begin to dilate allowing more blood and nutrients to the irritation. White blood cells begin to arrive to fight off invading substances. Inflammation thus develops. This in part sets the stage for healing.

However, these same forces if ignored and not treated will begin to break down body tissue allowing further irritation and causing destruction of skin cells. If this is continued to be ignored, severe infection results and eventually septicemia develops which can kill the baby.

Nothing outside the baby causes the destruction, except the invasion of the body by bacteria which may be with the baby during its whole life. The self actualization tendency to heal has actually turned on the baby and killed it. The baby self destructs.

When proper intervention is given in the form of diaper change, washing, Vaseline or A&D ointment applications, the self actualization tendency is maximized and healing can take place. As long as someone outside of the baby takes charge and provides care, healing can occur. Without the help, self destruction is maximized.

Fromm's position is more socially and psychologically oriented than this dealing with aggression, cruelty, and destructiveness.

Rogers seems to fail to acknowledge self destruction. He acknowledges the maximization of the self actualization tendency. However, he does not acknowledge the maximization of the self destruction tendency.

Further, Rogers by claiming that human nature is basically good has been called naive.

"There is abundant evidence to show that factors unavailable to consciousness motivate behavior, and that what a person says of him or her self is distorted by defenses and deceptions of various kinds. Self-reports are notoriously lacking in reliability, not only because people intend to deceive their listeners, but also because they do not know the whole truth about themselves" (Hall & Lindzey, 1978, pp. 303-304).

This argument seems to have a flavor of the evil side of the human experience even if that evil seems to be a little bit of the "little white lie" syndrome. It seems clear in Rogers' emphasis on the goodness of the human experience and on unconditional positive regard that he fails to acknowledge the significance of the evilness of the human experience. The closest Rogers' comes to acknowledging self destruction seems to be in this statement. "The actualizing tendency can, of course, be thwarted or warped, but it cannot be destroyed without destroying the organism" (Rogers, 1980, p. 118).

Rogers' side-steps the evidence which is supported by a rich tradition which is established theological and psychological circles. From the Genesis "Fall", to the Psalmist's "all righteousness is as filthy rags, to Paul's "all have sinned and fall short of the glory of God," to Luther's (1977) "The Bondage of the Will", to Paul Tillich's (1975 & 1963) estrangement, to Freud's "death wish" to Jung's "shadow" to Menninger's (1973) "Whatever Became of Sin?", to Christopher Lasch's (1979) "The Culture of Narcissism", there has been a wealth of support for the self-destructive nature of human beings .

However, Rogers' by rejecting self destruction and emphasizing the goodness and self actualizing tendency of human beings does seem to be arguing against the perversion or over emphasis on the evilness of human beings. His Congregational background would have been Calvinistic in thinking and he may have been exposed to a distorted view of this Calvinistic thinking which focused only on man as a fallen sinner who is incapable of doing anything constructive and who is totally deprived and alienated from God. Rogers correctly emphasizes the significance of the human being having the capacity to be growing, creative and responsible. He just seems to over react to the distortion that human beings are also evil by rejecting this evil.

Conclusion:

Rogers' Person-Centered theory is not beyond criticism. He and his followers do not seem to deal with criticism by being self critical or by assimilating criticism. However, thoughtful honest interaction which is relatively free of hero worship should lead one, at least, to hear the criticisms which are made about the approach.

It is my hope that I have listened and accepted the criticisms I have discovered about the Person-Centered theory that I might enter into significant dialogue with critics of this theory which I have come to appreciate and assimilate.

References

Bozarth, J. D. (1984). Beyond reflection: Emergent modes of empathy. In R. F. Levant, & J. M. Shlien, *Client-centered therapy and the person-centered approach: New directions in theory, research and practice*. New York, Praeger.

Bozarth, J. (1998). *Person-centered therapy: A revolutionary paradigm*. Ross-on-Rye: PCCS Books.

Bozarth, J. D., & Temaner, B. S. (1984). *Client-centered psychotherapy: A statement of understanding.* Unpublished Paper.

Fromm, E. (1973). *The anatomy of human destructiveness*. New York: Holt, Rinehart, and Winston.

Garfield, S. L., & Bergin, A. E. (1986). *Handbook of psychotherapy and behavior change*. New York: John Wiley & Sons.

Gurman, A. S., & Razin, A. M. (1977). *Effective psychotherapy: A handbook of research*. New York: Pergamon Press.

Hall, C. S., & Lindzey, G. (1978). *Theories of personality*. New York: John Wiley & Sons.

Lasch, C. (1979). *The culture of narcissism*. New York: W. W. Norton & Company.

Luther, M. (1977). *The bondage of will* (H. Cole, Trans.). Grand Rapids: Baker Book House.

Menninger, K. (1973). *Whatever became of sin?* New York: Hawthorn Books.

Raskin, N. J., Rogers, C. R., & Witty, M.C. (2008). Client-centered therapy. In R. J. Corsini, D. Wedding, & F. Dumont, (Eds.), *Current psychotherapies*. Belmont, CA: Thomason.

Rogers, C. R. (1957). The necessary and sufficient conditions of therapeutic personality change. *Journal of Consulting Psychology,* 21(2), 95-103.

Rogers, C. R. (1961). *On becoming a person*. Boston: Houghton Mifflin.

Rogers, C. R. (1977). *On personal power*. New York, New York: A Delta Book.

Rogers, C. R. (1980). *A way of being*. Boston: Houghton Mifflin.

Wolberg, L. R. (1977). *The technique of psychotherapy*. New York: Grune & Stratton.

Tillich, P. (1957 & 1963). *Systematic theology*, Vol. I & II. Chicago: The University of Chicago Press.

Implications of the Person-centered Approach for Pastoral Counseling

About 1984 I started a research project at Columbia Theological Seminary triggered by initial work on a Ph.D. at the University of Georgia. I was working on a Master of Theology in pastoral counseling at the time. The project was part of the requirements for completing the degree. I had been interested in discovering what therapy was. Having investigated several theories of counseling and psychotherapy, I found the Person-Centered approach to be the most congruent with who I am.

In the process I decided to develop under the supervision of Jerold Bozarth that looked at the attributes of a handful of adherents to the practice of the Person-Centered therapy.

During the project, I looked for a pastoral counselor to add to the list of recognized leaders in the Person-Centered approach. I could not find a single representative. I asked pastoral counselors who were familiar with the literature to recommend prominent Person-Centered colleagues, but they could produce no names even of a lesser-known colleague who claimed adherence to the Person-Centered approach.

This difficulty was unexpected, as Rogers is acknowledged as having a great deal of influence on the pastoral counseling movement in the fifties and sixties. His articles appeared in The Journal of Pastoral Care and Pastoral Psychology. His books were mandatory reading in seminaries and clinical programs. He was referred to by leaders in pastoral counseling and pastoral theological literature. Yet no Person-Centered pastoral counselor could be found.

Fuller (1984) that Seward Hiltner, Thomas C. Oden, Carroll A. Wise and Don S. Browning were influenced greatly by Rogers. However, neither Wise nor Browning appeared to maintain Rogerian concepts. I found only Oden, a pastoral theologian, to be a strong adherent to Rogers' views. Hiltner articulated an adequate definition of empathy, but he stopped short of addressing the process of being empathic. Browning (1976) noted that Hiltner's notion of "eductive counseling" is similar to Rogers' nondirective approach. Yet, the definition of "eductive counseling," implying the process of drawing out is quite dissimilar from the definition of empathy, which implies the process of entering into. Hiltner's "eductive counseling" is aimed at getting the client to do something, while Rogers' empathy is aimed at the only goal of the therapist, to enter into and perceive the world of the client as the client sees it, the client doesn't have to do anything at all except be himself.

What Happened?

It is clear there had been a courtship with Rogers, but there was never a marriage. Some pastoral counseling theorists may have engaged Rogerian theory, but there has never been a commitment to that theory. It appears that there has never been an assimilation of the theory as one's primary approach. Pastoral counselors have adopted psychoanalytic, TA, Gestalt and other theories; yet, although many have come to acknowledge Rogers' thought as significant, I found no Person-Centered pastoral counseling practitioner. I discovered years later that a minister by the name of Doug Land was an adherent to the approach, but I didn't find written material asserting his position.

Rogers was regarded as having tremendous potential for pastoral care and counseling. According to Fuller (1984), Rogers' nondirective approach offered ready assimilation in comparison with other approaches examined in pastoral counseling. "Client-centered therapy requires less formal training than other psychotherapeutic models . . . It can, therefore, be more easily introduced to seminary students and even full-time ministers whose schedules do not permit extensive psychological training" (p. 356).

On the surface, this claim would appear to be true. However, being empathic is not as easy as it appears, nor is understanding Rogers' concept of genuineness or any other aspect of the theory. Further, exercising acceptance and unconditional positive regard can be difficult. All require as intense a degree of interaction with Rogerian theory as practicing psychoanalysis does with Freudian theory. Regarding a superficial understanding of Rogers, Bozarth and Mitchell (1981) commented that "students and practitioners who believe that they are practicing the Client-Centered Approach . . . often have not learned the essence of this therapeutic effort. They are familiar with 'reflection' and with the importance of 'developing a relationship.' Too often, however, they equate the Client-Centered Approach to Human Relations Training Models. They view Client-Centered Therapy as only a prerequisite to other kinds of responding and miss the entire essence of the approach" (p. 1).

Further, Fuller (1984) stated that Rogers is easy to assimilate because the jargon is simple. "Rogers's writings employ less jargon and are thus more accessible to a general reading knowledge" (p. 356). He apparently feels Rogers is easily understood. However, there is a great deal of depth in Rogers' thinking that is frequently overlooked. He is often misread and his readers may often take it for granted that they understand the approach. Fuller himself admits this: "I would even go so far as to state that the vast majority of theologians who have studied Rogers's works have either misread or distorted the fundamental character of what might be labeled the broadly religious and spiritual thrust of his psychological writings" (p. 363). After spending over 27 years of grappling with Rogers' theory, I would go on to say there has been a significant failure to accept even the psychological aspects of his writings, despite the acknowledgment of the impact of Rogers in the psychotherapeutic field.

Where Does the Tension Lie?

The most obvious tension lies in what is viewed as the limitations of the approach. The conditions of empathy, acceptance and congruence may be regarded as necessary but not sufficient for growth. This is exemplified by Clinebell (1966), who adds the missing ingredients which he believes can complete the necessary and sufficient conditions:

"The Rogerian method provides a firm foundation but not the entire edifice of an adequate approach to counseling . . . The Rogerian model has tended to make the minister feel that he should strenuously avoid the use of his authority . . . In contrast, the revised model (which I propose) is based on the conviction that it is often constructive, even essential, for the pastor to use his authority selectively in sustaining, guiding, feeding (emotionally, inspiring, confronting, teaching5and encouraging persons to function responsibly" (pp. 30-31).

Another tension lies in a pessimistic skepticism a-bout the human condition, rooted traditionally on the theological influence of Paul, Augustine, Martin Luther, John Calvin and others. Mankind is made up of sinners who are incapable of doing good apart from the grace of God. Left to their own devices, mankind will continue to kill and maim fellow human beings. Left to their own devices, human beings will be destructive. They cannot be trusted:

"Beware the beast man, for he is the devil's pawn. Alone among God's primates, he kills for sport or lust or greed. Yea, he will murder his brother to possess his brother's land. Let him not breed in great numbers for he will make a desert of his home and yours. Shun him, for he is the harbinger of death" (Serling & Wilson, 1968).

Another tension rests in the perception of the authority of the pastor. Apparently, some pastoral counselors and pastoral theologians have felt this authority is threatened when the person-centered approach is adopted.

"The pastoral counselor, in adopting the strategies of client-centered therapy, risked blurring his or her distinct identity as a representative of the Christian church ....

> The exclusive use of client-centered or 'eductive' counseling techniques would, for example, appear to be a complete abdication of responsibility for confronting persons with the demands of moral and spiritual existence . . . A further concern . . . is that nondirective approaches to pastoral care and guidance ultimately lead to the impoverishment

of the sacramental, mystical, and contemplative elements of Christian spirituality. The utterly optimistic view of human nature upon which Rogers' theory rests is . . . inconducive to fostering attitudes that orient individuals to look beyond themselves in their search for meaningful existence" (Fuller, 1984, p. 360).

I believe that these criticisms slip into two categories. The first is a failure to accept the optimistic view of human nature. Rogers' theory is regarded as naive. This criticism fails to note Rogers' awareness of the difficulty and even the terror of the human situation.

"I would not want to be misunderstood on this. I do not have a Pollyanna view of human nature. I am quite aware that out of defensiveness and inner fear individuals can and do behave in ways which are incredibly cruel, horribly destructive, immature, regressive, anti-social, hurtful. Yet one of the most refreshing and invigorating parts of my experience is to work with such individuals and to discover the strongly positive directional tendencies which exist in them, as in all of us, at the deepest levels" (Rogers, 1961, p. 27).

The second criticism concerns the exercise of authority. Rogers is not anti-authority; he is anti-authoritarian. He does not believe in controlling others. Confrontation, direction, and pointing out discrepancies in behavior are manifestations of an authoritarian, "I am the expert" attitude (Bozarth, 1998). A vein of such authoritarianism runs through the history of the church and its clergy. What Rogers is interested in is personal power. One gains authority in the person-centered approach by being able to give up institutional authority and by recognizing and accepting the personal power of other persons.

A New Paradigm for Pastoral Counseling

The person-centered approach has more to offer than human relationship training. It addresses an enter dimension of being. I have seen nothing in the pastoral literature which is similar to Rogers' approach even though many claim to have been influenced by his thinking. "The concepts which are the crux of the person-centered approach and which reflect the very essence of a 'new age paradigm1 have been secondarily considered and barely mentioned in the literature" (Bozarth, 1985, p. 6).

The person-centered approach offers several principles of potential value to pastoral counseling. The first of these principles is that the presupposition of the process of the actualizing and formative tendencies - on the individual and the universal level - is the very foundation of the person-centered approach. "Rogers is explicit that the actualizing tendency, which is a characteristic of organic life; and the formative tendency, which is a characteristic of the universe as a whole '. . . are the foundation blocks of the person centered approach' (Rogers, 1980)" (Bozarth, p. 7).

The Person-Centered pastoral counselor would have a trust and faith in the self-actualizing capacity of the client. "Practice, theory, and research make it clear that the person-centered approach rests on a basic trust in human beings, and in all organisms" (Rogers, 1961, p. 117). Bozarth & Mitchell (1981) said, "The therapist must be able to act on the belief that the individual will move in the direction of self actualization when the therapist creates an atmosphere of acceptance and attends to the concrete-experiential flow of the client" (p. 3).

Such an attitude is pivotal to the Person-Centered approach: "The fact is that if therapists are not able to act on this belief then they are not practicing Client-Centered Therapy . . . It is essential that therapists have nearly unfaltering 'faith' that individuals, given the opportunity, will engage in an optimal mode of experiencing" (Bozarth & Mitchell, p. 3).

The second principle is that the locus of control lies with the client. Can the client be him or herself in the presence of the therapist? Can the therapist recognize the client's inner ability to move in a self directive way?

"Therapists often have difficulty being with their clients when the clients are 'muddled' or do not clearly communicate expected progress as perceived by the therapist. At the same time, therapist often seems patently unwilling to "allow" the client to be extremely sad or in pain or psychotic. Their misperception . . . in therapy is primarily the view the relationship can be developed in such a way that the therapist can then guide the client towards appropriate direction and action. Focusing on the therapist's authoritative expertise often becomes more important than creating the atmosphere which allows the client to achieve self-direction.

Many therapists assume that their competence and progress is judged relative to how able they are to motivate clients to address and resolve problems in living. Thus the client is viewed in terms of what 'ought to be discussed' or 'what the person should do' (i.e. in terms of the therapist as authoritative expert)" (Bozarth & Mitchell, pp. 3-4).

In the Person-Centered approach the emphasis is not on how astutely the counselor can predict or interpret behavior. The emphasis is on giving up the position of the power of the 'expert' in order to become empathic. There is a "willingness of the facilitator to give up institution 'position power1 for the opportunity to have personal influence, interaction . . ." (Bozarth, 1981, p. 119).

In relationship to the locus of control, the pastoral counselor in the Person-Centered approach does not presuppose anything about the direction of the client's progress. That is, the pastoral counselor does not presuppose how the client can 'get better.' The pastoral counselor accepts the client in his own "idiosyncratic way by only assuming the self-actualized tendency without presupposing what the client should do, or become, or be during or beyond the psycho-therapeutic encounter" (Bozarth, 1985a, p. 1).

The last principle pertinent to pastoral counseling is that the role of the pastoral counselor is that of having certain attitudinal principles or qualities: empathy, acceptance and congruence. To be true to the Person-Centered approach is to maintain a way of being, based on attitudes instead of techniques.

The therapist's role in the person-centered approach can be simply stated: Be real (genuine); be nonjudgmentally caring (unconditional positive regard); and enter the world of the client as if you are the client (empathy). Having these attitudinal qualities, the therapist 1) does not presuppose what a client might do, be, or become; and 2) has only one intention, i.e., to enter the world of the other "as if" he/she is the person. It is by the therapist being a person who has these characteristics that the client perceives the characteristics and personal growth is promoted" (Bozarth, 1985, p. 10).

Summary

The person-centered approach has ostensibly had an influence on the pastoral counseling movement. However, it as often been misread rejected or superficially understood. In as much as there are no significant leaders in the pastoral counseling arena that are Rogerian, the Person-Centered approach has not been assimilated.

Rogers offers pastoral counseling a new paradigm: 1) to trust and have faith in the capacity of the human being to move in a self directive way, 2) to give up the position of institutional authority and expertise and allow the locus of control to rest with the client, and 3) to maintain the attitudinal principles of empathy, acceptance and congruence (genuineness).

References

Bozarth, J. (1981). The person-centered approach in the large community group. In G. Gazda (Ed.), *Innovations to group psychotherapy*. Springfield: Charles C. Thomas

Bozarth, J. (1985). *Quantum therapy: The person-centered approach as an existing paradigm*. Unpublished manuscript.

Bozarth, J. (1985a). *A reframing of client-centered therapy*. Unpublished manuscript.

Bozarth, J. (1998). *Person-centered therapy: A revolutionary paradigm*. Ross-on-Rye: PCCS Books.

Bozarth, J., & Mitchell, S. (1981). *Functional dimensions of the person-centered approach in therapy*. Unpublished paper.

Browning, D. S. (1976). *The moral context of pastoral care*. Philadelphia: The Westminster Press.

Clinebell, Jr., H. J. (1966). *Basic types of pastoral counseling*. Nashville: Abingdon.

Fuller, R. C. (1984). Rogers's impact on pastoral counseling and contemporary religious reflection. In R. E. Levant, & J. M.. Shlien (Eds.), *Client-centered therapy and the person-centered approach*. (pp. 352-369). New York: Praeger.

Rogers, C. R. (1961). *On becoming a person*. Boston: Houghton Mifflin.

Serling, R., & Wilson, M. (1968*). Planet of the apes* [Film]. New York: Twentieth Century Fox.

Awkwardly Exploring The Paul Tillich – Carl Rogers Dialogue

Opening Comments

When I set out on this project, I had intended to approach the Rogers – Tillich Dialogue heuristically. I wanted to see what I could learn and pass on to readers. I found rather that I had a more critical interaction than I had anticipated. For what it's worth, I pass on those observations in this chapter.

A Brief Personal Background

While studying nursing at Manatee Jr. College in Bradenton, FL in the late 60s, I received a superficial exposure to Carl Rogers. I was taking a required course on Interpersonal Relationship Training.

During one of the classes the director of the nursing program came to the class and made a brief presentation. As she offered points on her take on the Rogerian approach to IPR, one of the students began asking questions about the approach. He sounded rather skeptical to me.

The professor and the student interacted. The student became frustrated during the interaction as he expressed his skepticism. The intensity of his responses grew and escalated. He sounded angry to me.

The professor kept repeating parts of what the student said. It was that old unfortunate model of virtually parroting what the other person was saying.

And then suddenly, the student's demeanor changed. I don't remember if I thought he thought he had been had, or if he had an "ah-ha" experience. He suddenly sat down and said no more.

My perception of the approach though from that point on was about repeating what was said to the listener back to the person who said it.

It was not until the early 80s that this changed. I took a course with Jerold Bozarth and the University of Georgia on theories of counseling and psychotherapy. I had up until that time a narrow minded view that the psychodynamic/psychoanalytic view was the only real kind of therapy. Yet, I never really could get fully immersed in the skill of interpretation and the methods involved with this area.

In some ways it was rather fun to interpret the behaviors of others. However, I often found myself out of sync with the interpretations of colleagues regarding clients. I often was even more out of sync with the interpretations of supervisors in relationship to me. Sometimes they were right on target and even triggered cathartic experiences and personal revelations. Other times they were so off target to me that they felt invasive.

When I got a chance to line up various theories, primarily using Corey (1982), I found that my basic behavior was very congruent with the person-centered approach presented by Carl Rogers. Also, I felt it was very helpful to study with a person who was committed to the approach rather than giving lip-service to the approach in lectures.

I began to embrace the approach. I felt my own reputation grew as I began to meet a host of contributors to the approach, Fred Zimring, Barbara Brodley, Bob Lee, John Shlien, Nat Raskin, John Woods, Chuck Stuart and others. In addition, I was developing a network of peers in Carol Wolter-Gustafson, Dave Spahn, Regi Roberts, Lisa Register, Ann Glauser, Elizabeth Strickler, Jo Cohen Hamilton, Paula Bickham, Howard Ellis, Jeff Penick, and Dottie Coleman among others.

For a number of years I was pretty fundamental with the approach though I harbored doubts about the basic goodness of human beings, unconditional positive regard, nonjudgmentalness, and nondirectiveness. I was also reluctant to call myself person-centered.

My doubts exploded in my own mind leading to reclaiming a position that while human beings are good, there is an evil in human behavior that leads to war, crime, and oppression. I was not willing to attribute that to influences from society alone. Also, I saw some pretty mean behaviors exhibit themselves among the person-centered community and began to doubt that unconditional positive regard was really practiced and with it nonjudgmentalness. And then I began also to see the insistence the real person-centered practitioners be nondirective as a form of directiveness. I replaced some of these concepts and addressed them within the community, especially on the Internet ad nauseam.

I now see the approach radically differently than I did when I was first exposed to it in the late 60s.

My exposure to Paul Tillich was far more flabbergasting. Tillich is far too left brain oriented for my right brain functioning. I had the opportunity to tackle some of Tillich's thinking at Columbia Theological Seminary in Decatur, GA as I studied with Ben Kline. Dr. Kline's reputation at the seminary was one of being an expert on Tillich.

I remember writing a paper for the course I took and expressing some dismay that Tillich had a reputation as a womanizer. Being a rather self-righteous judgmental person at the time, I was aghast at this and was pretty hard on Tillich in that paper. I am pretty sure in that, I missed a great deal of what Tillich had to say.

Now, I couldn't point to where I saw that tabloid type reputation and certainly can't vouch for its accuracy.

I am far from being an expert on Paul Tillich. I am still too right brain oriented to deal with his material. He is too abstract for me, but when I can cut through that abstractness, I rather like what I can grasp of the concepts of the "courage to be" "ground of being" and "ultimate concern." I wouldn't have the audacity myself to attempt to explain these concepts here or any where myself. They represent a different intellectual paradigm than the one in which I function.

In the late 80's, early 90s, I was exposed to Howard Kirschenbaum's (1989) work, Carl Rogers: Dialogues. It features interactions with

Tillich, Skinner, Bateson, Polanyi, and May. While I have had the material in my personal library for nearly 20 years, I only read the interaction with Rollo May. My exploration of that was related to the basic condition of human kind as being good and/or bad. I essentially reclaimed a position I had shelved that human kind is both.

However, in the last few months, that is late 2008 and early 2009, I began re-exploring the quest for the historical Jesus material. I had viewed that quest through mythological glasses. I perceived it has dismissive rather than affirming of faith. It has been my experience there is truth in my perception. However, Schweitzer whom I had seen as a ring leader in this skepticism was not as friendly to the quest as I thought. I also discovered the writing of Martin Kahler. Writing in the late 1890s, I found he was raising issues and questions concerning the quest for the historical Jesus that were similar to my own.

Paul Tillich wrote the Forward to one of the translations of Kahler's work "The So-Called Historical Jesus and the Historic Biblical Christ." During Carl Braaten's Introduction in that work, Rudolf Bultmann's name came up.

Having read Bultmann several times and struggling with his concept of "demythologization"decided to revisit Bultmann. I have a copy of Geoffrey W. Bromiley's (1981) work dealing with letters between Karl Barth and Rudolf Bultmann. I worked my way through that material. I experienced them as awesome.

In this pilgrimage, the name of Paul Tillich kept appearing.

So in this circular pilgrimage is a rationalization of dealing with the Rogers-Tillich dialogue.

Several years ago, I attempted to get an audio copy of the dialogue for a colleague in Greece. However, the copy was of such poor quality that I couldn't justify sending it.

Recently, I was able to improve the quality by transferring it to an electronic form. I found that a film version is available on the Internet. Thus, all that work was for naught. There are better recordings available. At this writing part 1 and part 2 of the Rogers - Tillich dialogue is available for viewing at http://www.carlrogers. info/video.html. However, as quickly as Websites change, this source may not be accessible in a few years. It is presently associated with the Archives, at the University of Santa Barbara, California.

This is the easy part, sharing my pilgrimage. The hard part follows for to go there I will be moving into left brain activity that I don't feel as comfortable with.

The Lost Introduction

Sometime ago, I solicited a recording on behalf of a colleague in Greece concerning the dialogue between Paul Tillich and Carl Rogers over an Internet network to which I belonged. Someone had a copy that he sent me. I don't remember who that person was, but I got a copy of the dialogue on a micro cassette. I needed a cassette tape recording and did not have the equipment to transfer the material to such a tape. Thus, the tape sat in my desk drawer for a number of years.

When my own interests peaked as the result of personal studies, I revisited the tape. It turned out to be of poor quality. It was also recorded at the wrong speed. Having obtained a cassette recorder for recording at slower speeds, I transferred the material from the micro cassette to a traditional cassette. Then I sped up the recorder to play the sound at what would have been a normal flow of conversation.

This actually only verified the poor quality of the material.

However, there were a few minutes of monologue on the tape that apparently has not been captured in transcript form. The tape is of such poor quality that there is no information as to its source. It would be great to offer specific information for citation. However, that information is missing. The introduction is not noted in several sources of the Tillich/Rogers interaction: (Kirschenbaum & Rogers, 1989); (Saybrook, 2006); (Cooper, 2006).

[Garbled] "The world renowned philosophical theologian at a conference arranged by members of our staff here at San Diego in March 1965. I was out of town when the conference started, but returned in time to hear some of his talks. When I arrived back in town I was asked if I would interview Dr. Tillich in front of the conference audience. I agree because I felt if I could draw out Paul Tillich the person this would probably be greatly appreciated by the conference members. This interview in front of a large audience was far from being a success by my standards. Dr. Tillich had excellent statements to make to each of the questions that I asked or in regard to the comments I made. However, each of the statements that he made seemed highly abstract as though drawn from some reservoir of speeches or essays which he had presented in the past.

My reaction to the interview was well summed up by a member of our staff who said to me afterwards, in a somewhat mournful tone, 'well, that was a good try Carl.'

The next day San Diego State asked if Dr. Tillich and I would converse with one another in front of TV cameras. I determined that I would divert to make it more of a dialogue hoping to us to draw them out more. I felt that these two dialogues were much more successful. And some of the significant personal points of view of each of us, I think, are contained in the two have our conversations which we held."

Carl Rogers followed this with a few comments on technical aspects of the TV interviews. There appeared to be no particular material relative to either Carl Rogers' or Paul Tillich's theories.

Rogers did take note that Paul Tillich died a few months later and the interview was his last public appearance.

Personal Comments on the Lost Introduction

It is well known that the person-centered approach with Carl Rogers being the premier advocate of the approach has held several premises: unconditional positive regard, nondirectiveness, and nonjudgmentalness.

It occurred to me as I listened to Carl Rogers' introduction that he held the reputation of Paul Tillich in high esteem. After all, agree or disagree with him personally, Paul Tillich had a major impact on Theology and Philosophy before and after World War II. This influence continues into the new millennium.

The principle of nondirectiveness though was abandoned. Carl Rogers said, "I felt if I could draw out Paul Tillich the person this would probably be greatly appreciated by the conference members." I found myself believing this was the genuine Carl Rogers who was indeed willing to "draw out" someone. Yet, this contradicted my perception of his commitment to nondirectiveness. Rogers also seemed patronizing. Paul Tillich was a public figure who rubbed shoulders with the likes of Karl Barth, Rudolf Bultmann, Reinhold Niebuhr, and a host of others. It is doubtful that Carl Rogers needed to "draw" him out. Rogers' position essentially says that Tillich withheld himself from audiences. How one would determine that far more complicated than one or two public interviews?

Not being a fan of nondirectiveness, I at least appreciated this hope that Rogers had. I wonder though why apparently he was not, nor are many of his followers willing to apply this kind of directiveness to clients. Do they feel they violate clients, but not people like Paul Tillich when they behave this way? I would think it was actually be the opposite. One would facilitate the drawing out of clients, but enjoy the genuineness of the widely respected person.

Also, I was struck by Rogers presupposing that the audience would appreciate his efforts to draw out Tillich. It was reported that the audience was full. People had come to hear Paul Tillich earlier, and then Carl Rogers and Paul Tillich. In a sense, to actually be in the auditorium would be an awesome experience. It would not be surprising with that many people that there would have been those who were disappointed. They might have been disappointed in Tillich, or Rogers, or Rogers' effort to draw out Tillich, or both men.

This leads me to the next violation of the approach, the premise of nonjudgmentalness. Rogers said in his introduction, "each of the statements that he made seemed highly abstract as though drawn from some reservoir of speeches or essays which he had presented in the past.

"My reaction to the interview was well summed up by a member of our staff who said to me afterwards, in a somewhat mournful tone, 'well, that was a good try Carl.'"

First, I haven't seen a lot of evidence pointing to Carl Rogers having read much of Paul Tillich's material. His own material never triggered an "ah-ha," Tillich said something like that response in me. Nor, did I see any evidence that Rogers attended presentations, lectures, or sermons by Paul Tillich. Thus, I personally experienced a sense of Rogers' judgmentalness about Tillich being abstract. I have seen nothing by Tillich that wasn't loaded with abstraction. So my sense is, what you see is what you get. The drawn out Tillich is an abstract thinker.

Also, I don't of a clue what "well, that was a good try Carl" means. It reeked with disappointment from these advocates of nonjudgmentalness.

Hereto, I don't have a lot of room for nonjudgmentalness and consistently find myself hoping and wishing that adherents would stop using the term. However, it is doubtful it will disappear.

I am though satisfied that Carl Rogers had great respect for Paul Tillich. This respect transcended the directiveness and judgmentalness I felt I saw from Rogers. However, I am not prepared to say this was unconditional positive regard. Would Carl Rogers have been willing to meet with others for such a dialogue who did not have the reputation of Tillich? Certainly, he did so for demonstration purposes many times. And just as certain, there was only so much of Carl Rogers to go around, thus limiting his personal ability to offer positive regard to people anyway.

I submit that unconditional positive regard is so limited that it is no longer useful. Accepting what one can, the way one can do so, has to be sufficient, regardless of regard.

I am left with two persons of great reputation who had a moment in history together. Their reputations made it special. Their presence, their capabilities, and their talents made their reputations possible.

In the scheme of things, only a tiny percentage of people even wanted to visit this event where two intellectual giants came together. Even fewer even made that visit, with even fewer remembering what was said. Some of us will enjoy the awe and wonder of their meeting which may include really not liking what was said and being disappointed.

I for one feel I saw a side of Carl Rogers that was not congruent with his premises. I saw a genuine Carl Rogers whom I felt was judgmental.

I also felt I saw a genuine Paul Tillich. So I don't believe that "Well, that was a good try Carl" captured anything but disappointment.

Now the Hard Part: Gleaning Through
the Tillich-Rogers Dialogue

The dialogue is available elsewhere (Kirschenbaum, & Henderson, 1989), among other sources. So I want to get at my thoughts and experiences as I go through the material for the first time. This is consistent with the way I approach material. I trust my responses, especially the errors. I learn something. I find that these often trigger responses in others, even if that response is to tell me how incorrect I am. I also trust the interpretations I have for they may facilitate different interpretations in others.

I predict, since I am writing this section before I explore the formal Tillich-Rogers dialogue, that I won't be able to present all the material I want to present. The dialogue probably has far too many points to address.

Also, I want to take into consideration that both Rogers and Tillich probably said things I wont understand. There simply will be too much complexity for me to deal with.

They also probably said things that I won't even consider worth commenting on.

The reproduction of the dialogue will encumber this article. My source for that dialogue will be the one reproduced in (Kirschenbaum & Henderson, 1989).

What I Observed (Or How I Responded)

Rogers opened the dialogue by speaking to "self-affirmation" and the "courage to be." He asserted that the two concepts held some commonality. As a naive reader imagining that I was in the audience, I found myself already uninformed. What is self-affirmation? What is the courage to be? How are they the same? I experienced ignorance. Is the concept of self-affirmation presented by a humanist (if I dare place Rogers into that arena), really consistent with the concept of the "courage to be" presented an existentialist)? I heard no exploration of the concepts. Thus, the comparison was beyond my grasp.

I also didn't understand what Rogers meant by the terms "logical positivistic," "ultra scientific approach," "mechanistic," and "deterministic." I didn't learn what they meant for Rogers or Tillich.

However, I did feel that the heart of his concerns with the above terms was the dehumanization of human beings. The human being is "just an object" under these perceptions.

While, I am not a fan of the Rogerian term "nondirective," I believe that the term is indeed about empowering people and thus respect the humanity through respecting the potentials of human beings to resolve their own problems. Where I believe the term falls short is the person coming to another for help is seeking to expand his or her own resources to deal with one's personal world. In short, the client coming to another for therapy, may indeed be seeking fresh ideas and has the capability of rejecting any or all of those fresh ideas regarding finding resolution for person problems.

Tillich essentially concurred with Rogers that they were in agreement. However, I didn't learn from Tillich what the concepts above meant to him. Tillich (2000) presented the two concepts ("self-affirmation" and "courage to be") together. A major theme of that work, as (Schilken, 1997) noted was "courage is the strength to continue to live on in a meaningful way in spite of the fact that our existence appears to have no purpose. We do not wallow in doubt, self-derision or despair. We have come into being in this time, in this place, in spite of the ever-present threat of non-being." Would this be in sync with the concept of self-actualization? Somehow the person drawing on personal resources thrives via a host of psychological, social, and yes spiritual levels to both exist and function as a unique person among other unique persons.

The "Overview" (Google, 2009) of Tillich's (2000) work on Google asserts the work, "describes the dilemma of modern man and points a way to the conquest of the problem of anxiety."

Tillich's own (2000) comments are in relationship to Spinoza's version of humanism, not Rogers. That focus doesn't have the positive slant that Rogers has of the human situation. I learned early from Corey (1982) that Rogers' view of human nature is a positive one. Tillich's view is about angst.

Thus, the agreement stated by Tillich escapes me. I am not convinced that the self-affirmation of Rogers, or the courage to be of

Rogers' that of Tillich. In fact, Tillich wrote, "Modern humanism is still humanism, rejecting the idea of salvation. But modern humanism also rejects renunciation" (p. 19). Indeed, with Rogers (1986) there is no need for salvation and renunciation runs counter to the concept of nonjudgmentalness and unconditional positive regard. Rogers then would be consistent with Tillich's description of Spinoza's position. If in this description we see Tillich's position, then Rogers and Tillich are in agreement. However, it is not reflective of Tillich's position who speaks about issues of estrangement. If one is estranged, there is room for some sort of salvation, internal or external in relationship to that estrangement.

Affirming that there was agreement Rogers moves in another direction. There is nothing like agreement to stifle interaction.

In apparent agreement, Rogers moved to explore his own uncertainties. He sought to deal with the "nature of man." He did so in part by extending a query to Tillich about his perspective on the issue. Quickly, he presented a presupposition that existentialists hold that man has no nature.

Such a position never occurred to me. Can the human being who has fallen into existence, engages or avoids angst, and is considered an ontological entity, not have a nature? Can there by existentialism without ontology, even if there are disagreements or contradictions in expressing thoughts, ideas, and presuppositions on the positions espoused in the midst of existentialism? Thus, can existentialism assert that man has not nature?

Rogers then speaks of his view that man belongs to specific species and shares the characteristics of those species. For instance, we also share characteristics with gorillas, apes, and other primates. One is hard pressed to point to what makes human beings so different from these other creatures.

Then, while not at all intending to speak to this, Rogers asserts that man tends to move towards actualizing one's self. Actually, this can be said of the animals as well. Yet, in this Rogers asserted that man's nature can be describable.

Rogers then wanted to explore Tillich's position on the "demonic aspects of man." With this, I felt Tillich was being baited. It is well known that Rogers held the goodness of man. My own exposure to that came with Corey (1982). It was reinforced uncounted times during my personal pilgrimage with the person-centered approach. One of my favorite sources of this was a Rogers (1986) article.

It is also well known that Tillich (1967) had room for a more negative view of human nature. He had a positive view as well. Rogers was either naive, or insincere in his query.

I think I would have felt differently about this section had Rogers spoke of his view of the 'nature of man' and then inquired about Tillich's. The contrast would quickly be revealed. Instead, I felt one had to already be familiar with Rogers' position.

In Tillich's response to Rogers, he quickly affirmed the existence of the "nature" of man. While he pointed to Sartre as an existentialist who denied that man has a nature, Tillich asserted that man's freedom to "make himself" is itself a nature. Tillich thus denied that one can deny the nature of man.

Tillich stated that he perceives two natures in man. The first is his true or essential nature. He moved theologically towards presenting this true nature as a created nature. This nature was created "good." He supported that from the creation epic of the first chapter of Genesis. He also supported the theological position by drawing from Augustine.

Tillich acknowledged the conflict in the early Church over this issue. I was personally surprised that he limited that acknowledgment to the early Church. Perhaps because there is such a strong emphasis on the depravity of man which is marked by sin characterized by corruption, vanity, and personal or spiritual poverty among other descriptions (Calvin, 1960). This is pretty accepted in the contemporary Church and lead to Rogers (1986) comments.

The negative may overwhelm Tillich's affirmation of the true nature of man being good. Here Rogers' position and Tillich's are in agreement. It probably is safe to say that the congruent person is basically good. It may also be safe to say that this is true of the incongruent person, that person's basic nature is good.

Tillich though ventures to the second nature (an existential nature) as "mixed." This mix is the "accepting" and the "distorting" of one's true nature. Man finds the self as estranged from one's true nature. Man contradicts the true nature. For Tillich this nature is very human and without it, man wouldn't be man. However, as real as it is, Tillich saw it as a distortion of the essential nature.

I found myself wondering though if this existential nature was absent, would the human being in a state of total essential nature be human. While this is an ideal state, surely the human being could be fully the self one truly is without the mix that Tillich presented. That may be part of Tillich's position. The real person, the real human presently has this "mix" as part of the nature of man and cannot escape it.

This position seems in sync with Rogers' concept of incongruence.

In the dialogue, Tillich offered to go into a third position. However, Rogers again entered the dialogue moving from listener to presenter. Personally, I have to do so often during interactions for if I wait to make a point, I forget what I responding to, or what my point is.

He expressed what has become one of my favorite positions in the person-centered approach. In my words, it is the position of being open to whatever the direction the client takes. Rogers holds that in this openness rather than the client choosing to move in "evil" or "antisocial" ways, the client moves in directions of "self-understanding" and "more social behavior."

On this aspect, I am not in agreement. I found people getting in touch with their despair, anger, ability to be hurtful and harmful, and anxiety. I remember one of my mentors asserting that the child abuser might become a better child abuser. I found this troubling. I am personally not interested in facilitating a person's path to finding creative and resourceful ways to hurting others.

Instead, I found myself taking a position of being open to the possibility that a client may indeed move in "evil" or "antisocial" ways. Yet, I also found that with continuous or consistent offerings of the core conditions of empathy, acceptance, and genuineness, the client was more likely to move in the directions that Rogers addressed.

I am more convinced that the absence of the "core conditions" is more likely to foster "antisocial" and self destructive behaviors (Bower, 2000).

Rogers essentially addressed the issue of freedom whereby the therapist creates an environment of freedom being open the self directiveness.

Tillich though questioned whether a person is free enough to create such an environment. He thus appeared not to have a place of what Rogers would call congruence. The existential person is in a constant state of alienation from the self and wouldn't be able to escape enough from that state to enter into such freedom. If the therapist isn't really free to be fully the essential nature, how could he/she be free to create freedom for another.

In this, Tillich spoke to the "ambiguity of life." This ambiguity arises out of the dichotomy of the essential nature and the existential nature. Perhaps, to say it arises out of the tension between the self one truly is and the distorted self might capture some aspect of the ambiguous.

I experienced myself wondering, first, how marvelous it is that Paul Tillich being a man of profound reputation, in relationship with Carl Rogers of equal reputation in a differing field, was in a position to raise issue with Rogers on the issue of freedom. Over the years acquiesced to the giants in my life and did not feel comfortable with questioning their positions. Then second, I wondered if the use of the word freedom was a distraction on the issue of creating an environment that Rogers has long espoused. Is being open to the direction a client takes really about freedom? Perhaps being open to those directions are about legalism from time to time. Good person-centered therapists are open to the direction that client's may take. One is supposed to behave in such a manner. That doesn't sound like freedom, but obligation.

Tillich saw this "predicament" as universal. He thus, differs from presuppositions of Rogers about the nature of man as Rogers does have room for a fully functioning person (Rogers, 1961). Tillich's position has a great deal of room for what has been called through the years as evil. Tillich (1967) may have in some way spoken about this in relationship to his concept of "new being." However, neither person entered into these concepts at this point in the dialogue. However, Tillich stated, "so I am more skeptical, both about the creation of such a situation and about the individuals who are in such a situation" (p. 68).

I think this supports that unfortunate use of the word freedom by Rogers. As above, it is probably more of an issue of being open to the directions the client may take. This then would be or could be conceived as a freedom to get at the human predicament this client is experiencing. So the word "freedom"may not be so unfortunate as to not use it all. Perhaps freedom is really freedom when one is free to be broken. However, if one becomes broken, can one have the freedom to no longer be broken?

Rogers augmented his position a bit acknowledging that creating an environment of "complete freedom" was difficult. However, he didn't back away from his belief that a person in an environment of acceptance and understanding seems "to liberate the person to move toward really social goals" (p. 68).

He then inquires about Tillich's position on the demonic.

Tillich first addressed where he felt there was some agreement with Rogers. He saw some importance for love in the formative years of children. However, he left a very interesting question unanswered. "Where are the forces which create a situation in which the child receives that love which gives him, later on, the freedom to face life and not to escape from life into neurosis and psychoses?"

For me, I revisited believing that the absence of love, or in the case of the person-centered approach, the absence of the core conditions, is all too real in life. The escape into neurosis and psychoses is related to that absence (Bower, 2000).

Tillich then makes a brief dive into his concept of the demonic. In doing so he spoke of his contact with the psychoanalytic movement in the 1920s and its impact on "changing the climate of the whole century" (p. 69). It would be interesting if he had developed what that change was about in this section of his dialogue.

He also addressed briefly the impact of Karl Marx, but did not elaborate on that impact either.

In this, he asserted that traditional concepts of the "fallen" or "sinful"nature of man are somehow inadequate to address the changes in relationship to Freud and Marx.

Personally, I felt this showed his bias because I have not trouble myself using those terms in relationship to either Freud or Marx: with Freud, because his assertions concerning the "Id" which has an aspect of selfishness, greed, and self-centeredness; and with Marx, because of his assertions concerning oppression and domination by the elite social classes over the lower classes.

Tillich felt the term "demonic" was more appropriate. He affirmed its connection with New Testament stories of Jesus. It was "similar to being possessed"(p. 69). There is something within the individual that interferes with the ability of the person to be a person of "good will." In this, he denied a mythological component: "little demons or a personal Satan running around the world" (p. 69). Rather, this demonic is ambiguous, destructive, and is part of the estrangement of mankind. The demonic takes hold of a person leading to conflicts in class, and society. Even efforts to overcome them seem to drive people deeper into the demonic.

Rogers responds to the issues of alienation and estrangement by utilizing infants as an illustration. He asserts that infant is not estranged from himself.

I agreed and disagreed with Rogers. I have long trusted that when an infant was crying it was crying out in sync with itself. There is something wrong. When an infant is cooing, it is in sync with itself. The infant is content.

However, I disagree in the sense that a cry out of hunger sounds the same as a cry about pain in the foot. The estrangement from the self rests in not yet being able to access the way to accurately communicate what hurts. Further, there is estrangement from others. The infant was moved from a nice warm wet environment, into a bright, maybe colder, dry environment. Sounds are different. Experiences are different. The infant can even make his/her own sounds. In short, the infant is in process of discovering how to function and is often out of touch with how to stop crying when conditions change. I am convinced that infants might be able to stop cooing quicker than they can stop crying.

Rogers continued speaking to the infant's path towards adulthood and his/her encounter with the significant others, probably parents, in regards to love, judgments, and other psycho-social experiences.

I found it interesting that Rogers used the term "bad boy, bad boy" in his dialogue on these issues. Rogers illustrates this, "In other words, he has introjected the notion that he is bad, where actually his enjoying the experience . . ." (p. 70). This of course assumes that he is enjoying the experience. What if as he enjoys experiences, he hits a little girl when he gets older? Or, what if he appears to be enjoying an experience, but it is a misinterpretation by Rogers that the experience is satisfying. There appears to me a glimpse of the issue of nonjudgmentalness as important to the conditions for growth that Rogers long espoused. Also, it appears to me to a glimpse at the cause of estrangement from one's self which is also part of the Rogerian position. The impact of this judgmentalness is scantily dealt with in Rogers (1957). Judgmentalness is not traditionally received in the approach as a "good" state for persons to be in.

Could it be though that a person raised in a nonjudgmental environment, if that were possible, might have his/her own kind of estrangement and incongruence? I would assert yes. One being so nonjudgmental would be living in a very lonely place. I am not very sure that the world would be very friendly to such a person.

In response Tillich states "the infant is a very important problem" (Kirschenbaum & Henderson, 1989, p. 70). He compares the infant to Adam and Eve before the Fall. He called this "dreaming innocence." The reality of the infant's being has "not yet reached reality." Tillich noted that "the Fall" does not reflect as closely this state of dreaming innocence as does this psychological jargon. For Tillich the dreaming innocence of the infant and the Fall mean the same. For him there is a process of movement away from dreaming innocence or the Fall to "conscious self-actualization." In the midst of this, estrangement occurs.

At this point, I agreed with Tillich when he said, "I agree with you that there is also in what the parents used to call 'bad boy' or 'bad girl,' there is a necessary act of self-fulfillment, but there is also something asocial in it, because it hurts his sister and so it has to be repressed, and whether we say 'bad boy' or prevent it in anyway, this is equally necessary . . ." (pp. 70-71).

Certainly Rogers is correct. There is a thwarting of the self in this act. Yet, Tillich is correct as well. The person cannot be allowed to hurt another. That part needs to engage the resistance of a society that frowns on hurting others. Tillich recognized the tension in the movement from dreaming innocence to self-actualization as well as the estrangement that occurs.

This does not strike me as consistent with Rogers who espouses that a nonjudgmental stance liberates the person towards more social behavior. As much as I agree an environment can help facilitate movement towards more social behavior, I also resist the notion in part because I believe there is the possibility of a laissez faire attitude which would also facilitate asocial behavior. This laissez faire attitude was not condoned by Rogers (1951). My own impression of the approach in general is laissez faire may be deliberately or non-deliberately advocated in the staunch nonjudgmental emphasis of the approach.

Rogers begins a response by saying, "there is much that I would agree with" (Kirschenbaum & Henderson, 1989, p. 71). It would be great to explore where he thought the agreement was. I personally think there is agreement with Rogers' concept of incongruence, and Tillich's concept of estrangement. However, Tillich, as noted above, is not as optimistic about estrangement being overcome. Rogers is optimistic about incongruence being overcome. Certainly, anyone dealing with the interview could state where he or she thought agreement rested. What is missing is where Rogers thought the agreement was.

Rogers moved from this brief statement to what he believes bring healing to the estranged incongruent human person. The "courage to be" or the "tendency to become oneself" for Rogers is seen as occurring only in a relationship. He asserted that acceptance of the unacceptable aspects of oneself can only occur in an accepting relationship. This triggered a connection with my understanding of Rogers (1957a) hypothesis on the "necessary and sufficient conditions" for therapeutic change.

Rogers said, "This, I think, is a large share of what constitutes psychotherapy - that the individual finds that the feelings he has been ashamed of or that he has been unable to admit into his awareness, that those can be accepted by another person, so then he becomes able to accept them as part of himself" (Kirschenbaum & Henderson, 1989, p. 71).

What is unclear to me is if this acceptance amounts to condoning what was previously seen as asocial or antisocial behavior. For instance, does the discovery that a person abuses children become acceptable? I have been in dialogues with person-centered colleagues who appeared to me to condone the child abuse. Fortunately, I haven't seen such affirmations in the literature I have explored. However, on the personal level charges of being judgmental have been levied towards people who expressed concern about a person abusing children. I myself, find I am willing for a client to speak to the issue of abusing children. I am unwilling to give the impression that child abuse or other antisocial behavior is condoned.

Tillich affirms Rogers' stance on the importance of acceptance as "necessary" for "self-affirmation." He added the word "forgiveness" to this acceptance.

This helped me add a new twist to my concept of "forgiveness." I have traditionally viewed the concept as a setting aside of the consequences regarding personal, moral, ethical, or legal violations. A person might over look the insult of a friend or another person instead of lashing back. Or a judge might decide, based on evidence and circumstances, to drop charges with the cooperation of the prosecution. The strong Biblical flavor of forgiveness is to not even remember the violation. A more realistic Biblical flavor of forgiveness is not to impose judgment on the person committing the violation. It is hardly realistic to ask people to forget as part of forgiveness.

What Tillich added for me was seeing forgiveness as "acceptance of the unacceptable."

I thought though I heard Tillich say that one cannot accept oneself. This does not come out in the written dialogue recording by (Kirschenbaum & Henderson, p. 71). Rather, it came for listening to a recording I have of the tape. This is not to say it is impossible. It seems to be related to a proneness "to hate yourself" As long as that self-hate exists, then the inability to forgive oneself is diminished.

Here Tillich varies from Rogers who asserts this acceptance is about relationship. For Tillich holds the formal confessional rites of the Church, and probably other institutions, are important for something of :another dimension." Still, Tillich affirms that this is made possible by a relationship "from men to men."

Tillich though stated that he all but abandoned the use of forgiveness "because this often produces a bad superiority in him who forgives and the humiliation of him who is forgiven" (p. 71-72). I would assert though that should this be the case, this is not forgiveness. It is patronization. Forgiveness levels the "playing field," if I may use a common term. It creates equality, not disparity.

Tillich acknowledged that he preferred the word "acceptance." He saw it a very adequate term to update old presuppositions concerning forgiveness. Here he probably matches pretty well with Rogers' concept of unconditional positive regard: "the way in which the psychoanalyst accepts his patients, no judging him, not telling him first he should be good, otherwise I cannot accept you, but accepting him just because he is not good, but he has something within himself that wants to be good"(p. 72).

The use of the word "psychoanalyst" may indicate Tillich's limitation on what "psychotherapy" is about. Rogers (1986) position is hardly that affirming of the psychoanalytic perspective since he sees it as the psychoanalyst assuming the role of expert and thus creating the very attitude of superiority that Tillich was concerned about in relationship to the concept of forgiveness.

I doubt very seriously if the concept of acceptance really is all that immune to Tillich's concern about forgiveness. Surely, acceptance can come with this issue of superiority.

Rogers responded by asserting strongly his belief in acceptance. Here he noted that the "potency of acceptance" is demonstrated "when an individual feels that he is both fully accepted in all that he has been able to express and yet prized as a person" (Kirschenbaum & Henderson, 1989, p. 72).

My own explorations and experiences in the approach hold experientially that this holds true. However, I want to push it beyond prizing and positive regard. Can I accept the "negative?" Can I be open to my own experiences of negativity with the client, not necessary overtly expressing them, but taking note of them for what they are? Can I incorporate feelings of dismay, frustration, even anger, into the perceptions I have in relationship to another? Can I trust these experiences regardless of regard, positive, neutral, or negative?

Has acceptance been romanticized to only be associated with warm, fuzzy experiences? Has it been rationalized to be associated with believing in the person no matter what the person does?

Tillich responded to Rogers' notion of acceptance by stating that this acceptance is at the heart of the "good news" of the Christian message. Certainly, the traditional Christian song "Just as I am" confirms Tillich's assertion. It also seems, at least on the surface, to be compatible with Rogers' concept of acceptance.

Hereto the Christian message suffers from the same possibilities. It can be perceived so radically, and then when this acceptance is not present, the Christian faith comes into question. People are called hypocrites. What if this acceptance is not always a pleasant, positive experience? Can there be room for accepting that it feels awful to be human at times, and it feels awful to be a person of faith at times. Can it be seen as unpleasant for the therapist to be accepting of the client? Surely, clients have experiences of feeling awful, and their therapists feel awful about them. Is there room to include this in the manifestation of acceptance? Pushing it even further, is there room to accept "unacceptability?"

At this point in the dialogue there was break or "Intermission." I find myself staggered by the material addressed so far and wondering if it can hold together to be read.

Part II

When a double header is played in baseball, the second game can be completely reversed from the first game. So, before approaching the second half of this dialogue I quickly wondered what might be different.

Tillich kicked off the second session by speaking about the minister as a representative of "the ultimate meaning of life." There was no development of what that means. So, based on this, one is left without an explanation.

He linked this with the "unconscious skills" of this minister. While having skills, the minister, being "unskilled" should not attempt to be a "second rate psychotherapist." This is unclear. However, since Tillich referred to Freud earlier, it may not be far fetched to think he had psychoanalysis in mind. In this, I wondered how much psychotherapy had been mythologized to be only for the trained psychoanalyst. Certainly, I don't believe untrained people should be psychotherapists in any discipline. However, there is more helping going on in the world that leads to productive change than takes place in psychotherapy. If not, the world is in worse shape than we have been led to believe. There aren't enough psychotherapists within all the disciplines to of help. Other forms of help are essential.

I am tempted to say that Rogers demythologized psychotherapy and counseling. That in part may have been why he had such severe critics. The conditions he espoused as therapeutic can be found in some neat people in the world who are teachers, grandparents, priests, nurses, etc. If therapy is the restructuring of the self (Rogers, 1961), then restructuring might take place in a synagogue, school classroom, on a walk in a park, or in a hospital room. It cannot be limited to the domain of Psychoanalytic, Gestalt, Cognitive Behavioral, or Person-Centered therapy. Certainly those with who focus on the practice of offering formal counseling, psychiatry, or psychotherapy need to be licensed.

When Rogers responded I saw something of him that I long suspected, but couldn't quite put my finger on. That is, he was raised in a traditionalist, fundamental Congregationalist household. He made a trip to China in that mind set that changed his life and his theology. I have long felt that his position is very much influenced by Christianity. However, he was also powerfully influenced by humanism. In this, he felt that discarding traditional Christian language would be very appropriate. I have no way of knowing if Rogers discarded his faith with discarding the Christian jargon. Nonetheless he said to Tillich: "I realize very well that I and many other therapists are interested in the kind of issues that involved the religious worker and the theologian, and yet, for myself, I prefer to put my thinking on those issues in humanistic terms, or to attack those issues through the channels of scientific investigation" (Kirschenbaum & Henderson, 1989, p. 72).

While studying at Southern Baptist Theological Seminary in Louisville, KY, I took a nursing position in a local hospital. There I got the first taste that there were psychotherapists who blamed religion as a major cause of mental illness. The person-centered approach in spite of Rogers attitude above has hardly been friendly towards people of faith. I have seen some pretty mean-spirited discussions in person-centered community meetings about religion. I among others learned to keep my mouth shut about some of my traditional values as a person of faith.

Still, personally, I appreciate Rogers' position on this. I have found the conditions representative of the intent of the Christian faith in particular. I do not feel qualified to speak about how representative of other traditions it might be. I suspect very much so.

Rogers then addressed the "God is dead" theme that was stirring at the time. I haven't heard it dealt within years. I had a bumper sticker on my car that read: "My God is not dead. Sorry about yours." I have investigated that theological position several times, but have never really felt I got a handle on it. Rogers seemed to hold a notion that was similar to the one I got hold of, but which I didn't then and still don't appreciate. He said to Tillich "religion no longer does speak to people in the modern world" (p. 72). He was not alone in that then, or in 2010. The like of Borg (2001), hold similar positions. The issue of irrelevancy of religion remains. Yet, D'Souza (2007) has taken note that Christianity is the fastest growing religion in the world. If he is wrong about that, I suspect that Islam has to be considered. The Rogerian approach in America at least has declined as a movement, even though Rogers has been acknowledged as having influenced counseling and psychotherapy more than any other theorist. I suspect Freud probably has had more influence even if it an influence that triggers rejection of his ideas. That of course is a bias. One would be hard pressed to remove Freud, Skinner, and the Cognitive Behavioral theorists from the realms of the top spot. At any rate, Rogers had blinders on when he spoke about faith and religion in such a manner.

Rogers offered Tillich a challenging question. As to why Tillich still put his ideas in "religious terminology." Before, I find out Tillich's response, my own is to answer saying, because Tillich doesn't share Rogers' view that religion no longer speaks "to people of the modern world." In fact religion does so even better than Rogers did. Even though Rogers had a great impact, there are a lot of people who never heard of him who have heard of major religions. Humanism in general has excited people, but it has also dismayed people, as has religion. The assumption that "religion no longer speaks" to modern people was and is grossly inaccurate.

I return to Tillich.

Tillich points to what he called two metaphorical dimensions. He saw a "horizontal dimension" in which the human being connects with the self and with others. He also spoke of a "vertical" dimension in which the human connects to the "infinite, unconditional, ultimate."

The horizontal dimension is finite, limited and comes and goes. He does come close though in joining Rogers in the claim that "religion no longer speaks" to the modern person. "I don't speak here - I must emphasize this in speeches again and again - in terms of life after death, or in other symbols which cannot be sued in this way anymore . . ." (p. 73). Instead he speaks to the "immediate experience of the temporal," the temporal impacted by the eternal. He saw that as a way of interpreting the "traditional religious symbols."

As an observer, I am not in a position to understand what Tillich meant here. I am in a position to understand he saw something different about his interpretation. I also feel he believed it was congruent with contemporary trends, probably around the world. I am also in a position to say that no matter what Tillich meant, his jargon and interpretation are hardly mainstream positions. The traditional jargon, at least of the Christian faith, strongly continues even in the face of trends that are dismissive of faith (Borg, 2001; Dawkins, 2006; Harris, 2004; Hitchens, 2007; Spong, 2001). Given that we are all limited and our world view tends to attract the similar (Rogers' notion of what is most personal is most universal), it is often easy to assume this a common view. I certainly have to apply that to what I have just said about my own observations. I do think there are a lot more regular people in the world attracted to traditional jargon about religion than there are regular people attracted to Rogers and Tillich. The Bible still remains at the top of the all time best seller list for a reason and it hardly was written in Rogerian, or Tillichian jargon.

Tillich though does hear that humanism as captured very succinctly in Rogers comment sees religion as "irrelevant." He thus acknowledges in his own way, what I just indicated above. There are people who "live in" the traditional where "preaching, religious teaching, and liturgies." He felt that those "estranged" from the traditional "need a translation and interpretation of this symbol" of the traditional. However, he felt Rogers was seeking a replacement" of the traditional. Maybe Tillich was correct in his interpretation of Rogers. However, I felt that Rogers was saying that estrangement from the traditional isn't the point. Rather, change was the point. The contemporary human being has moved away from even wanting the traditional and finding it inadequate for describing existing and being. Thus, self actualization, trust of one's potentials, and moving in socially positive directions are more important to human beings.

Should I get this point accurately at all, I feel I need to point out that Rogers (1986) uses this very philosophy to indicate how the person-centered approach differs from both psychoanalytic and Christian world views. It certainly also contrasts the flavor of contemporary forms of psychotherapies which hold the therapists as the expert (Bozarth, 1998). I tend to believe this contrast supports a position that the world view of Christianity and other religions really hasn't changed so much as to be seen as generally irrelevant.

Tillich closed his section saying, I hope playfully, "but we poor theologians, in contrast to you happy psychologists, are in the bad situation that we know the symbols with which we deal have to be reinterpreted and even radically reinterpreted. But I have taken this heavy yoke upon myself and I have decided long ago I will continue to the end with it." And indeed he did having died not long after the dialogue.

That is what theology does and has done through the ages; reinterpret the faith to a new generation. Those reinterpretations are sometimes embraced and sometimes rejected as being terribly incorrect even causing offense. This too sounds like the impact of the Person-Centered Approach.

But before leaving this section with its mild focus on the irrelevance of traditional religion in the contemporary world, while Rogers went to China on a missionary trip holding a traditional Christian jargon and abandoned it, Tillich though using a nontraditional jargon did not always abandon the traditional jargon (Tillich, 1955).

Rogers responded to Tillich's vertical dimension with a fantasy. The vertical instead of going up, comes down. Yet, something didn't quite match for me. I didn't really see an up and down in Tillich's vertical dimension coming from Tillich. It might be implied by the word. Rather, I simply saw a metaphor of difference. Something else felt more important to me than the up and down slant of Rogers' fantasy. Rogers spoke of being "in-tune" with the client who has come seeking help. Of particular importance to me was that he used the phrase "rare moments." I have long held myself that empathic experiences are actually rare, sort of like peak relationship experiences where the therapist gets so focused that he/she can almost speak for the client and may even say something about the client before the client says it. In these moments Rogers described them as being occasions where operating in the therapists are forces of the universe coming together to be utilized. There seemed to me to be a flavor of awe in Rogers' statement. He likened what he experienced to that scientist who can split the atom while not being the one who created the atom. He can participate in an encounter with the atom that can bring about change. The therapist does not create a client, but can participate in the path of the client uses to recreate him or her self. Something new comes from that which is old but is new be virtue of it being reshaped, not created.

Tillich connected with the up and down aspects of Rogers' comments. He pointed out that he had been accused himself of focusing on the down part of the vertical to the expense of the up part. He acknowledged that in his discussions or interest in the ultimate concern" he speaks of the "ground of being." This "ground of being" is down for Tillich, not in the sense of down being inferior in some way, but is the sense of metaphor. It is a different place, but a solid place (if I should be so bold as to say that). It is related to the depth of the universe and certainly as rich. From the "creative ground" comes form and elements. Certainly, this is not all that far from Rogers' (1960) discussion on the "formative tendency," "actualization tendency," and "self-actualization."

Tillich was in agreement that what he described as "creative ground" and its depth has an impact of "person-to-person" encounters. The jargon was simply different in that Rogers used the phrase "forces in the universe."

In addressing what I called "awe" Tillich recalled something related Thomas Aquinas' theology: "If you know something, then you know something about God" (p. 75).

I experienced both Tillich and Rogers being in awe.

Rogers next sought to explore a different issue. He described it as an issue of "what constitutes the optimal person" (p. 75). This optimal person 1) moves towards "greater openness to experience;" 2) is "more able to listen to what's going on within himself;" 3) is "more sensitive to the reactions he's having to a given situation;" 4) is "more accurately perceptive of the world around him;" 5) is "realistic about what is going on within himself, as well as realistic about the world;" and 6) becomes "more social." This is a very succinct and congruent presentation of Rogers (1951) understanding of the process of therapy. It is also consistent with Rogers (1961) view of the "fully functioning person."

Tillich responded with two questions. He called one "the way." He called the other "the aim." He related that he felt "familiar" with the issue of "openness." In this, he saw symbols functioning as a means of opening up reality and something of oneself. He used word "soul" as being in relationship to this inner self. However, in this he said, "if this word were not forbidden in the university, I would call it something in our soul, but you know as a psychologist, as somebody who deals with the soul, that the word 'soul' is forbidden in academic contexts" (p. 76).

I was concerned by that. Tillich just used the word "soul" before a sophisticated assembly. That he perceived that the word was "forbidden" spoke loudly to me. The man saw atrocity in Nazi Germany, yet he was hesitant to use a religious word in America. Was there a glimpse here of oppression, not just irrelevancy of religion but a deliberated thwarting of religion by forbidding certain jargon.

Still, he used the word "soul." There did not appear to be any consequences for his use of the word. However, he still spoke of the taboo.

He reflected briefly on experiencing God or getting to "the divine spirit," saying that one does so by keeping oneself open. "You cannot force God down, you cannot produce the Divine Spirit in yourselves, but what you can do is open yourselves, to keep yourselves open to it" (p, 76),

Tillich stated that he agreed with Rogers about openness.

I doubted it. The two are coming from different places. Openness for Rogers is openness to self, and society. He did not speak about being open to discovering God. Rogers was thinking of the secular. Tillich though was coming from the sacred, or the spiritual. He was coming from the opposite direction. Being open to oneself for Tillich, potentially, is being open to discovering God or the Divine Spirit. For Rogers, openness is self discovery. For Tillich, God might be discovered.

In regards to "the aim," Tillich indicated "aim" is 1) "realization of our true self;" 2) "bringing into actuality what is essentially given to us;" 3) "to become the way in which God sees us, in all our potentialities;" and 4) "to become more social."

For Tillich this related to "agape." The person is accepted by a person who has attempted to reunite with another in order to overcome "existential separation." Tillich further associates this with "faith," "ultimate meaning of life," in relationship to the "ultimate aim of life." Again, Tillich's understanding of this is theological, not psychological. He did see in this an "affirming of the other person, and oneself." "I wouldn't use the term 'self-love' - that's too difficult - but self-affirmation and self-acceptance, one of the most difficult things to reach" (p. 77).

Apart from the theology and the differences that are not easily addressed with secular ideologies, there is common ground here between Tillich and Rogers. I felt both men were getting at speaking to similar issues on estrangement/incongruence, acceptance, and openness. That one pointed to human beings as the final end and the other to discovering God as the final end somehow almost didn't matter. Or perhaps speaking to how it does matter, would take away from the interaction these two men had.

Rogers picked up on the themes of faith and love, but highlighted the person liking oneself. He associated this as a self-affirmation "in a healthy and useful fashion."

Rogers also pushed further on being "open to experience." This open person is constantly in a "valuing process." There is a valuing of "each moment" and of one's "behavior in each moment." This in turn is related to the person's self actualization and is related to the "mature person." Rogers also indicated a preference or believe that legalistic (my term) values from the past are probably not "appropriate or meaningful" as in the past.

Of the later statement, I found some danger in holding it too literally. There still remains value in not stealing, cheating on one's spouse, or killing the convenient store clerk, or beating one's dog. How far Rogers' statement goes remains a matter of debate. I have had colleagues at conferences say that they thought it was OK to have sex with clients, while even the American Psychological Association considers such behavior unethical. The fact of the matter is that while there is debate over what behaviors should be condoned or condoned, what is valued is not completely in the hands of any given person. There are other perspectives and ideologies that come into play.

Tillich reacted in support of values asserting that he himself was "an outspoken critic of the philosophy of values." I suspect both men were referring to rigid legalism that is all too often used as a club. Tillich believed that this should be replaced with "agape, or love" with love being connected to listening. The listening leads to decisions for "action" and inner "satisfaction." In this there can be "joy."

Rogers affirmed the listening stating it is about listening within, to oneself, and for the other person.

This triggered my own position on empathy. The basic concept is that of entering the world of another as if . . . . The "as if" aspect of empathy is too broad to explore here. However, I have long held (Bower, 1985) that one of the ways the therapist has a deeper understanding of the client is when the therapist experiences the same kinds of feelings that the client experiences. For instance: anger, hope, joy, sadness, etc. The therapist doesn't act out these feelings, though he or she might express them within the ethical guidelines of the profession. There is some legalism here. The therapist cannot go around doing whatever he or she wants to do because of his/her feelings in association with the client. Rather, I speak of using the feelings as a barometer or indicator of what the client is experiencing.

I find this informative not destructive. It becomes destructive when the therapist violates the principles of the person-centered approach. The alternative is to remain aloof and distant in the name of being objective and thus losing a valuable sense of knowing that comes with experiencing.

Tillich captured something that I feel is related to the position I just stated. "When I say listening to the situation, I mean the situation is constituted out of everything around me and myself, so listening love is always listening to both sides" (p. 78). I add that when I listen to me, I can also listen to the client. If I detached from the client, and only listen to me, then I miss the client. I need to allow the client to impact me as I enter the client's world. When that happens, provided I am not defensive, frightened, disrespectful, or lose control of myself, I can learn something about the client.

Rogers revisited the infant's experience of fully experiencing one's self in context of others. "I feel that the small infant is a good example of the valuing process that is going on continuously. He isn't troubled by the concepts and standards that have been built up by adults, and he's continually valuing his experience as either making for his enhancement or being opposed to that actualization" (p. 78).

That is true at the cognitive level. However, the person-centered approach has placed a great deal of emphasis on being nonjudgmental. If I stick to the infant as a "good example," I haven't met an infant yet that wasn't judgmental as hell. When an infant is crying, whether hunger, or a dirty diaper triggers the cry, that is a statement of "I don't like this!!!!!"

I have met many infants that experienced what they experienced in spite of the intellectual judgmentalness of the adults in their lives. So infants can have feelings which run contrary to the feelings of their care givers. Infants experience what they experience. That part, we may all wish we had more access to as we grow older.

Tillich said (and this astounded me as I have been writing this as I have read the material), "Now, this valuation, of course, would be not an intellectual valuation, but an evaluation with his whole being" (p. 78).

Rogers responded by saying, "I think of it as an organismic valuing process" (p. 78).

Finally, I share these words from Tillich. Both men have an approach for wholeness, genuineness, completeness. The infant illustrated that completeness. I was moved by them not because of content. They were the last words he spoke at a public forum. "That means a reaction of his whole being, and I certainly believe that it is an adequate description" (p. 78).

References

Borg, M. J. (2001). *Reading the Bible again for the first time: Taking the Bible seriously but not literally.* New York: HarperCollins Publisher.

Bower, D. W. (1985). *Assumptions and attitudes of the Rogerian person-centered approach to counseling: Implications for pastoral counseling.* Unpublished Research Project, Columbia Theological Seminary, Decatur, GA.

Bower, D. W. (2000). *The person-centered approach: Applications for living.* San Jose, CA: Writers Club Press.

Bozarth, J. (1998). *Person-centered therapy: A revolutionary paradigm.* Ross-on-Wye: PCCS Books.

Cooper, T. D. (2006). *Paul Tillich and psychology: historic and contemporary explorations in theology, psychotherapy, and ethics.* Macon, GA: Mercer University Press.

Calvin, J. (1960). *The institutes of the Christian religion* (J. T. McNeill, Ed., & F. L. Battles, Trans.). Philadelphia: The Westminster Press.

Corey, G. (1982). *Theory and practice of counseling and psychotherapy.* Monterey, CA: Brooks/Cole Publishing Company.

Dawkins, R. (2006). *The God delusion.* New York: Houghton Mifflin.

D'Souza, D. (2007). *What's so great about Christianity.* Washington, D.C.: Regnery Publishing.

Google. (2009). *Overview: The courage to be.*

http://books.google.com/books?id=xnw6zW2MXNgC&dq=ina uthor:Paul+inauthor:Tillich&lr=&as_drrb_is=q&as_minm_ is=0&as_miny_is=&as_maxm_is=0&as_maxy_is=&as_ brr=0&source=gbs_navlinks_s.

Harris, S. (2004). The *end of faith: Religion, terror, and the future of reason.* New York: W. W. Norton

Hitchens, C. (2007).*God is not great: How religion poisons everything.* New York: Hachette Book Group.

Kirschenbaum, H., & Henderson, V. L. (1989). *Carl Rogers dialogues.* Boston: Houghton Mifflin.

Rogers, C. R. (1951). *Client-centered therapy.* Boston: Houghton Mifflin.

Rogers, C. R. (1957). Personal thoughts on teaching and learning. Merrill-Palmer *Quarterly,* 3 (Summer), 241-243.

Rogers, C. R. (1957a). The necessary and sufficient conditions of therapeutic personality change. *Journal of Consulting Psychology,* 21(2), 95-103.

Rogers, C. R. (1961). *On becoming a person.* Boston: Houghton Mifflin.

Rogers, C. R. (1980). *A way of being.* Boston: Houghton Mifflin.

Rogers, C. R. (1986). Rogers, Kohut, and Erickson: A personal perspective and some similarities and difference. *Person-Centered Review,* 1(2), 125-140.

Rogers, C., & Tillich, P. (2006). *Carl Rogers and Paul Tillich #1 & - (1960)* Rogers and theologian Paul Tillich. San Francisco: Saybrook Graduate School & Research Center. http://www.carlrogers.info/video.html

Rogers, C., & Tillich, P. (2006). *Carl Rogers and Paul Tillich #2 - (1960).* San Francisco: Saybrook Graduate School & Research Center. http://www.carlrogers.info/video.html.

Schilken, R. (1997). Book Review: The Courage to be by Paul Tillich. http://blogcritics.org/books/article/book-review-the-courage-to-be/

Spong, J. S. (2001). *A New Christianity for a new world: Why traditional faith is dying and how a new faith is being born.* New York: HarperCollins.

Tillich, P. (1955). *The new being.* New York: Charles Scribner's Sons.

Tillich, P. (1967). *Systematic theology: Three volumes in one.* Chicago: The University of Chicago Press.